Alfred's Self-Teaching Basic Ukulele Course

The new, easy and fun way to teach yourself to play

RON MANUS • L. C. HARNSBERGER • NATHANIEL GUNOD

Playing the Ukulele

Playing the ukulele is more than just fingering a few chords and strumming some strings. Sure, it will bring music into your apartment or home, but it can do so much more than that. For many of us, listening to or performing music brings joy, pleasure, and relaxation into our lives. To put it simply, it's a lot of fun. It can take away, for a short time at least, the cares and tensions caused by problems we all face.

After a while, you will be able to play and sing for friends and even perform in beginning music ensembles. Many students quickly progress to the point where they can perform at parties. At Christmas time, you will be able to perform "Jingle Bells," and that is included. Fairly soon, and sooner than you might think, you will be able to perform for audiences of all kinds. The more you get involved with music, the more interesting and exciting your life can become.

What makes this course even more special are the unique Study Guides that precede most every music page. The Study Guides offer explanations, directions, and additional information to help you to more easily understand how to play. You also learn a little music theory, a little music history, and about songs and their composers. So much invaluable information is packed into the Study Guides. They become, in fact, your at-home teacher, assuring you of a quicker, more successful and enjoyable learning experience. You will always progress more quickly with a teacher, and if you use this book with a teacher, you will progress even more quickly.

About the CD and DVD

The CD enclosed contains a recording of every song title in the book. Listening or playing along with the recording is not only fun but also helps to reinforce musical concepts such as rhythm, dynamics, and phrasing. A DVD is also available that includes video demonstrations of every lesson.

Right now, there is one thing you share with Bruce Springsteen and Taylor Swift. They both had to begin—and that's what you are about to do. So turn to page 4 and let's get started.

Alfred Music Publishing Co., Inc.
P.O. Box 10003
Van Nuys, CA 91410-0003
alfred.com

ISBN-10: 1-4706-2363-3 (Book & CD)
ISBN-13: 978-1-4706-2363-0 (Book & CD)

ISBN-10: 1-4706-2364-1 (Book & CD & DVD)
ISBN-13: 978-1-4706-2364-7 (Book & CD & DVD)

Cover Photos
Ukulele photo by Jennifer Harnsberger
Man with ukulele: © iStockphoto / Jeanne McRight • Woman with ukulele: © Veer / Alloy Photography

 Alfred Cares. Contents printed on environmentally responsible paper.

Contents

Introduction

Study Guides

What makes this course special are the unique *Study Guides* that precede the music pages. The *Study Guides* offer explanations, directions, and additional information to help you easily understand how to play. You also learn a little music theory, a little music history, and about songs and their composers. So much invaluable information is crammed into the Study Guides. They become, in fact, your at-home teacher, assuring you of a quicker, more successful and enjoyable learning experience. You will always progress quicker with a teacher, and even more so using this book.

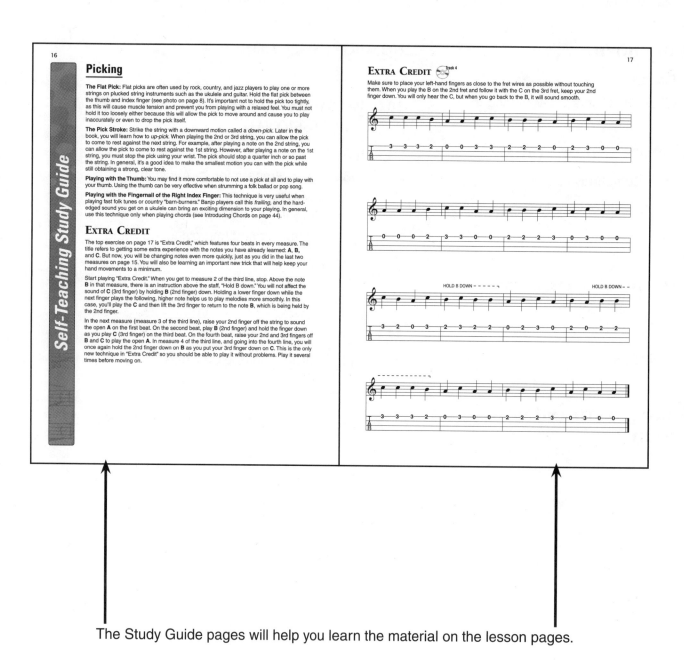

The Study Guide pages will help you learn the material on the lesson pages.

Selecting Your Ukulele

Ukuleles come in different types and sizes. There are four basic sizes: *soprano, concert, tenor,* and *baritone.* The smallest is the soprano, and they get gradually larger, with the baritone being the largest.

Soprano   **Concert**   **Tenor**   **Baritone**

Soprano, concert, and tenor ukuleles are all tuned to the same notes, but the baritone is tuned differently. Each ukulele has a different sound. The soprano has a light, soft sound, which is what you expect when you hear a ukulele. The larger the instrument, the deeper the sound is. Some tenor ukuleles have six or even eight strings.

The soprano ukulele is the most common, but you can use soprano, concert, and four-string tenor ukuleles with this book. If you want to play the baritone ukulele, use *Learn to Play the Alfred Way: Baritone Uke* (Alfred #380) to start learning.

The Parts of Your Ukulele

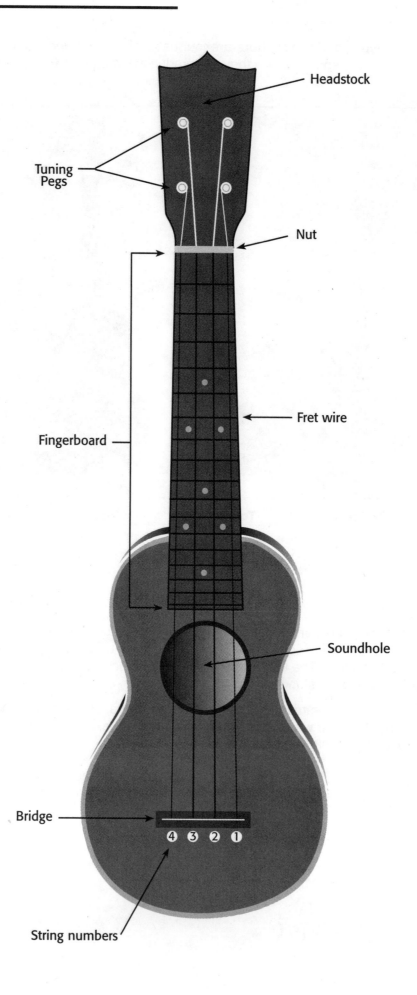

Headstock

Tuning Pegs

Nut

Fret wire

Fingerboard

Soundhole

Bridge

String numbers

How to Hold Your Ukulele

Standing

Cradle the ukulele with your right arm by gently holding it close to your body. Your right hand should be free to strum it. Keep your left wrist away from the fingerboard. This allows your fingers to be in a better position to finger the chords.

Sitting

Rest the ukulele gently on your thigh.

The Right Hand: Strumming the Strings

To *strum* means to play the strings with your right hand by brushing quickly across them. There are two common ways to strum the strings. One is with a pick, and the other is with your fingers.

Strumming with a Pick

Hold the pick between your thumb and index finger. Hold it firmly, but don't squeeze it too hard.

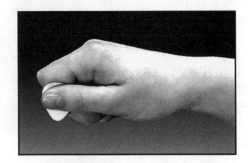

Strum from the 4th string (closest to the ceiling) to the 1st string (closest to the floor).

Important: Always strum by mostly moving your wrist, not just your arm. Use as little motion as possible. Start as close to the top strings as you can, and never let your hand move past the edge of the ukulele.

Start near the top string.

Move mostly your wrist, not just your arm. Finish near the bottom string.

Strumming with Your Fingers

Decide if you feel more comfortable strumming with the side of your thumb or the nail of your index finger. The strumming motion is the same with the thumb or finger as it is when using the pick. Strum from the 4th string to the 1st string.

Strumming with the thumb.

Strumming with the index finger.

Using Your Left Hand

Hand Position

Learning to use your left-hand fingers easily starts with a good hand position. Place your hand so your thumb rests comfortably in the middle of the back of the neck. Position your fingers on the front of the neck as if you are gently squeezing a ball between them and your thumb. Keep your elbow in and your fingers curved.

Keep elbow in and fingers curved.

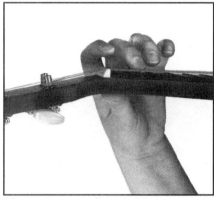

Like gently squeezing a ball between your fingers and thumb.

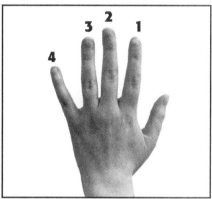

Finger numbers for the left hand.

Placing a Finger on a String

When you press a string with a left-hand finger, make sure you press firmly with the tip of your finger and as close to the fret wire as you can without actually being right on it. Short fingernails are important! This will create a clean, bright tone.

RIGHT
Finger presses the string down near the fret without actually being on it.

WRONG
Finger is too far from fret wire; tone is "buzzy" and indefinite.

WRONG
Finger is on top of fret wire; tone is muffled and unclear.

How to Tune Your Ukulele

Make sure your strings are wound properly around the tuning pegs. They should go from the inside to the outside, as in the picture below.

Tuning a tuning peg clockwise makes the pitch lower. Turning a tuning peg counter-clockwise makes the pitch higher. Be sure not to tune the strings too high because they could break!

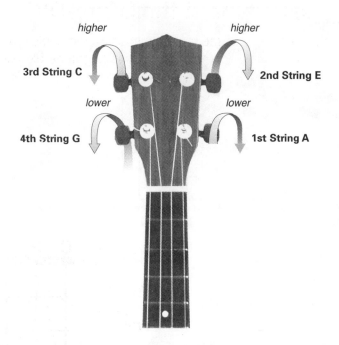

Important:

Always remember that the string closest to the floor is the 1st string. The one closest to the ceiling is the 4th string.

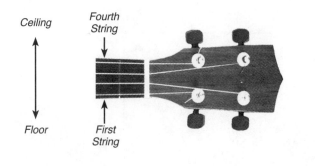

Tuning with the CD or DVD Track 1

To use the CD, play track 1. Listen to the directions and match each of your ukulele's strings to the corresponding pitches.

To use the DVD, go to the "Scenes" menu and click "Tuning." Follow the directions, and listen carefully to get your ukulele in tune.

Tuning the Ukulele to Itself without the CD or DVD

When your 1st string is in tune, you can tune the rest of the strings just using the ukulele alone. First, tune the 1st string to A on the piano, and then follow the instructions to get the ukulele in tune.

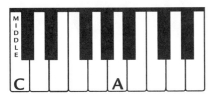

Press fret 5 of string 2 and tune it to the pitch of string 1 (A).

Press fret 4 or string 3 and tune it to the pitch of string 2 (E).

Press fret 2 of string 4 and tune it to the pitch of string 1 (A).

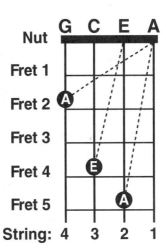

Pitch Pipes and Electronic Tuners

If you don't have a piano available, buying an electronic tuner or pitch pipe is recommended. The salesperson at your music store can show you how to use them.

Getting Acquainted with Music

Musical sounds are indicated by symbols called *notes*. Their time value is determined by their color (white or black) and by stems or flags attached to the note.

The Staff

The notes are named after the first seven letters of the alphabet (A–G), endlessly repeated to embrace the entire range of musical sound. The name and pitch of the note is determined by its position on five horizontal lines, and the spaces between, called the *staff*.

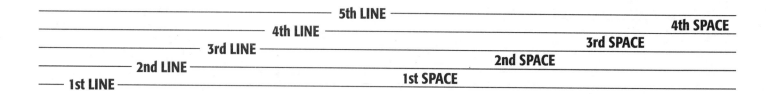

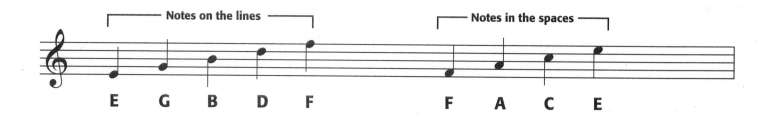

Measures

Music is divided into equal parts called *measures*. One measure is divided from another by a *bar line*.

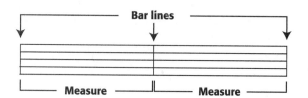

Clefs

During the evolution of musical notation, the staff had from 2 to 20 lines, and symbols were invented to locate certain lines and the pitch of the note on that line. These symbols are called *clefs*.

Music for ukulele is written in the *G clef* or *treble clef*.
Originally, the Gothic letter G was used on a four-line staff to establish the pitch of G.

This grew into the modern notation:

Reading TAB

All the music in this book is written two ways: in standard music notation and TAB.

Below each standard music staff you'll find a four-line TAB staff. Each line represents a string of the ukulele, with the 1st string at the top and the 4th string at the bottom.

Numbers placed on the TAB lines tell you which fret to play. A 0 means to play the string open (not fingered).

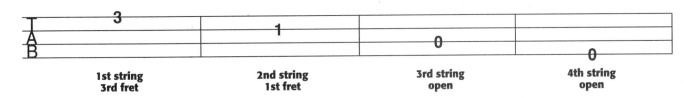

By glancing at the TAB, you can immediately tell where to play a note. Although you can't tell exactly what the rhythm is from the TAB, the horizontal spacing of the numbers gives you a strong hint about how long or short the notes are to be played.

Chord Diagrams

Chord diagrams are used to indicate fingering for chords. The example here means to place your 1st finger on the 1st fret, 1st string, then strum all four strings. The o symbols on the 2nd, 3rd, and 4th strings indicate to play them open (not fingered).

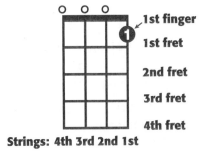

The First String A

A on the 1st String. Look at the top section of page 15. This section shows you three notes on the first string **A**. Let's start with the first diagram on the far left.

Finger Diagram. The words "open string" appear above the diagram, which is just like the chord diagram shown on page 13, and that means the **A** string is not fingered—it is just picked. This string is indicated as a solid line, while the other strings are dashed lines. Pick the solid line, not the dashed lines. The o above the diagram also means "open" (or not fingered).

As you hold the ukulele in playing position, the **A** string is the lowest (closest to the floor) and thinnest string on the ukulele though it is the highest in pitch. When ukuleleists refer to the highest string, they mean the highest-sounding string, the **A** string.

The Staff. Below the finger diagram is the five-line music *staff.* The first symbol you see is the *treble clef,* also called the **G** clef (see page 12). Counting *up* the staff from the bottom line, the note **A** is located *in* the 2nd space. Listen to the sound of the open **A** string by picking it with your right hand (RH).

B on the 1st String. The second diagram is for the note **B**. It is fingered by placing the 2nd (middle) finger just slightly behind the 2nd fret and pressing down just firmly enough to make a clear tone when you pluck the string. See the finger diagram to the right of the photo for the exact location of **B** on the fingerboard. Place your finger as close to the fret wire as possible without actually touching it. The music staff below the finger diagram shows that by counting up, **B** is located *on* the 3rd line. This is the note **B** played on the **A** string. Now finger **B** and pick with your RH several times. It should sound slightly higher than **A**.

C on the 1st String. The diagram and photo on the right is for the note **C**. It is fingered by placing your 3rd finger just behind the 3rd fret and pressing down just firmly enough to make a clear tone when you pluck the string. Once again, see the finger diagram for the exact location. The music staff below the finger diagram shows that **C** is *in* the 3rd space. This is the note **C** played on the **A** string. Now finger **C**, and pick with your RH several times. It should sound higher than **B**.

Music Exercise

Look down to the first line of music. To the left of the staff, you will see a finger diagram of the three notes and fingerings you have just learned. It is intended as a quick review.

The staff is divided into small sections called *measures*, and each measure is separated by *bar lines*—see page 12.

Begin by playing slowly and evenly. You can keep a steady beat in your head, or you can tap your foot. Each note is a *quarter note* and will receive one beat or tap of your foot. There are four beats in each measure.

The notes in measures 1 and 2 are all **A**'s, played on the open **A** string. The next two measures include all **B**'s, fingered just slightly behind the 1st fret. On the second line of music, measures 5 and 6 are all **C**'s, fingered just behind the 3rd fret. In measure 7, the notes change every two beats—**A** for two beats, then **B** for two beats. The last measure begins with two **C**'s, followed by a final **A** which is held a little longer, bringing the exercise to a close.

Play this exercise several times, saying the name of each note as you play. It is important to play the notes evenly and steadily. Do not stop between measures or between lines. Start slowly and gradually increase your speed.

PLAYING WITH A, B, C

The only new notation in the bottom exercise is the symbol at the very end. A thin line followed by a thick line indicates the end of a piece of music. This exercise includes only three beats in each measure. This will give you practice in changing notes a little more quickly. In the last two measures, you will be changing notes on every beat. That's quite an accomplishment after playing only one page. When you are comfortable playing this exercise, move on to page 16.

The First String A Track 2

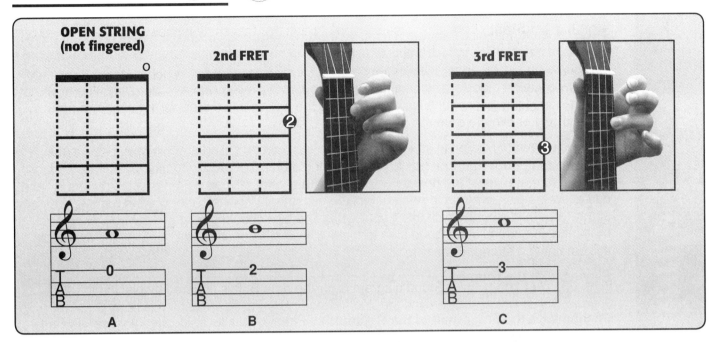

Play slowly and evenly. Use only down-strokes, indicated by ⊓.
The symbol ○ over a note means *open string*. Do not finger.

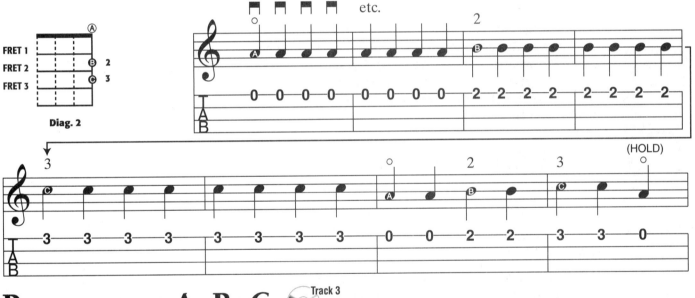

PLAYING WITH A, B, C  Track 3

DOUBLE BAR LINE

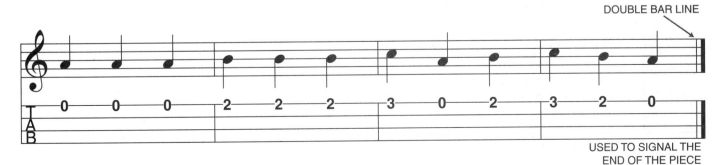

USED TO SIGNAL THE
END OF THE PIECE

Picking

The Flat Pick: Flat picks are often used by rock, country, and jazz players to play one or more strings on plucked string instruments such as the ukulele and guitar. Hold the flat pick between the thumb and index finger (see photo on page 8). It's important not to hold the pick too tightly, as this will cause muscle tension and prevent you from playing with a relaxed feel. You must not hold it too loosely either because this will allow the pick to move around and cause you to play inaccurately or even to drop the pick itself.

The Pick Stroke: Strike the string with a downward motion called a *down-pick.* Later in the book, you will learn how to *up-pick.* When playing the 2nd or 3rd string, you can allow the pick to come to rest against the next string. For example, after playing a note on the 2nd string, you can allow the pick to come to rest against the 1st string. However, after playing a note on the 1st string, you must stop the pick using your wrist. The pick should stop a quarter inch or so past the string. In general, it's a good idea to make the smallest motion you can with the pick while still obtaining a strong, clear tone.

Playing with the Thumb: You may find it more comfortable to not use a pick at all and to play with your thumb. Using the thumb can be very effective when strumming a folk ballad or pop song.

Playing with the Fingernail of the Right Index Finger: This technique is very useful when playing fast folk tunes or country "barn-burners." Banjo players call this *frailing,* and the hard-edged sound you get on a ukulele can bring an exciting dimension to your playing. In general, use this technique only when playing chords (see Introducing Chords on page 44).

EXTRA CREDIT

The top exercise on page 17 is "Extra Credit," which features four beats in every measure. The title refers to getting some extra experience with the notes you have already learned: **A, B,** and **C.** But now, you will be changing notes even more quickly, just as you did in the last two measures on page 15. You will also be learning an important new trick that will help keep your hand movements to a minimum.

Start playing "Extra Credit." When you get to measure 2 of the third line, stop. Above the note **B** in that measure, there is an instruction above the staff, "Hold B down." You will not affect the sound of **C** (3rd finger) by holding **B** (2nd finger) down. Holding a lower finger down while the next finger plays the following, higher note helps us to play melodies more smoothly. In this case, you'll play the **C** and then lift the 3rd finger to return to the note **B,** which is being held by the 2nd finger.

In the next measure (measure 3 of the third line), raise your 2nd finger off the string to sound the open **A** on the first beat. On the second beat, play **B** (2nd finger) and hold the finger down as you play **C** (3rd finger) on the third beat. On the fourth beat, raise your 2nd and 3rd fingers off **B** and **C** to play the open **A.** In measure 4 of the third line, and going into the fourth line, you will once again hold the 2nd finger down on **B** as you put your 3rd finger down on **C.** This is the only new technique in "Extra Credit" so you should be able to play it without problems. Play it several times before moving on.

EXTRA CREDIT  Track 4

Make sure to place your left-hand fingers as close to the fret wires as possible without touching them. When you play the B on the 2nd fret and follow it with the C on the 3rd fret, keep your 2nd finger down. You will only hear the C, but when you go back to the B, it will sound smooth.

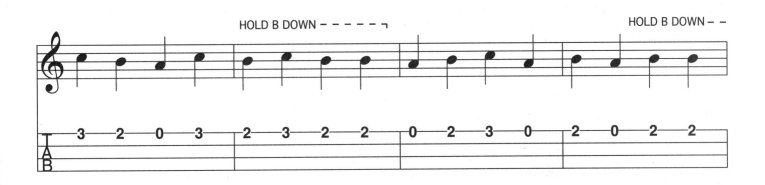

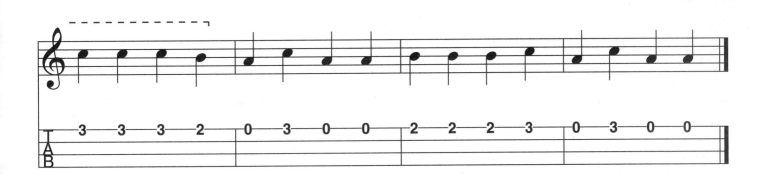

Sound-Off: How to Count Time

Now that you have become familiar with some of the notes on 1st string **E**, this seems like a good time to go into a little more detail about notes, the music staff, and a new term, *time signatures*.

The Quarter Note: At the top of page 19, there are four different notes displayed across the page. The first note on the left is the *quarter note*. That is the note you have been playing so far. As you know, it receives one beat or tap of your foot. There is a good mathematical reason it is called a quarter note, and we will get to that further down the page. Under the quarter note, you can see that this note receives one count. On your open **A** string, play **A** four times as you tap your foot and count evenly, 1–2–3–4. Each note you played was a quarter note. The quarter note consists of a solid note head (an oval) and a line extending up or down from it called a *stem*.

The Half Note: The note to the right of the quarter note is a *half note*. As you can see, each half note is held for two counts, or beats. Play **B** (2nd fret) on the **A** string and hold the note as you count, 1–2. Play the note again and hold it as you count, 3–4. Now, play this one more time without stopping, but this time tap your foot and count evenly: 1–2–3–4. You should have picked **B** on beats 1 and 3, holding the note for two beats each time. Each note you played is a half note. Notice the note head has a hole or white space within it.

The Dotted Half Note: The third note to the right is a *dotted half note*. A dot following a note increases the value of the note by one half. As a half note receives two beats, a dotted half note receives two beats (for the half note) + one beat (for the dot) totaling three beats altogether. This time, play **C** (3rd fret) on the **A** string and hold the note as you count and tap evenly, 1–2–3. That is the dotted half note.

The Whole Note: The last note to the right is a *whole note*. A whole note can be easily identified because it has no stem. It is held the longest of the notes you have learned so far, for four counts. Select any of the notes you have learned, play it, and count and tap evenly 1–2–3–4. That is the whole note. Like a half note, it too has a hole or white space within the note head.

Time Signatures

As explained on page 12, music is divided into equal parts called *measures*, or *bars*. One measure is divided from another by a bar line. About half way down page 19 and under the title Time Signatures, you will see a line of music beginning with two large 4s. The line contains two bar lines that divide the music into three measures.

Now read the paragraph under Time Signatures. Notice again the two large 4s at the beginning of the music staff. Those numbers are called the *time signature*. The top number tells you how many counts are in each measure; the lower number tells you what kind of note receives one count.

The first time signature shown is $\frac{4}{4}$ (or four-quarter) time. The top number 4 means we count the music in four, or four counts to each measure. The bottom number 4 means that a quarter note receives one count. At the top of the page, we mentioned there was a mathematical reason why a quarter note gets its name. Now you know the reason. It is because it takes up one quarter (¼) of the measure in $\frac{4}{4}$ time. A *half note* takes up half the measure, or two beats, and a *whole note* takes up the whole measure, or four beats. In $\frac{4}{4}$ time, the *dotted half note* receives three beats.

The next time signature on the page is $\frac{3}{4}$ (or three-quarter) time. The only difference between $\frac{4}{4}$ time and $\frac{3}{4}$ time is that now we count the measures in three, or three counts to each measure. Because the bottom number of the time signature is a 4, the quarter note still receives one beat, the half note still receives two beats, and the dotted half note still receives three beats. The whole note is not used in $\frac{3}{4}$ time. See the last measure of the music line beginning with $\frac{3}{4}$. The *dotted half note* takes up the whole measure, but it is not called a *whole note*. In $\frac{2}{4}$ time, we count just two beats in each measure.

Sound-Off: How to Count Time

Four Kinds of Notes

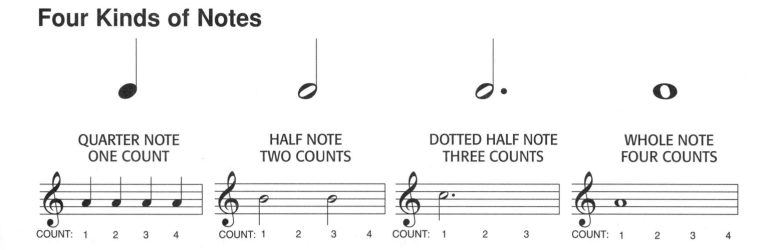

Time Signatures

Each piece of music has numbers at the beginning called a *time signature.* These numbers tell us how to count time. The TOP NUMBER tells us how many counts are in each measure. The BOTTOM NUMBER tells us what kind of note gets one count.

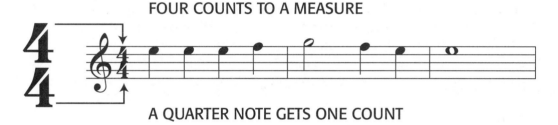

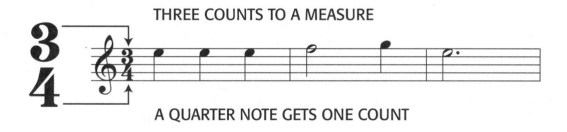

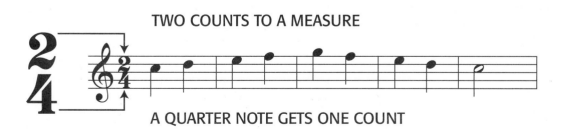

Important: Go back and fill in the missing time signatures of the songs already learned.

Repeat Signs

At the top of the next page is a section explaining *repeat signs.* A repeat sign is formed by two lines (one thick, one thin) with two dots placed either after the thin line (at the beginning of the repeated section) or before the thin line (at the end of the repeated section). It means to go back to the facing (beginning) repeat sign and repeat everything between the two repeat signs. In the example at the top of the next page, you would play two measures, then go back to the beginning and repeat the two measures, for a total of four measures.

1st String Blues

The blues is a truly American style that has its roots in spirituals that go back to before the Civil War. It is the foundation of jazz and rock 'n' roll. As you learn more notes and chords, you will be able to play more and more authentic-sounding blues music.

Notice the repeat signs at the beginning and end of "1st String Blues." When playing the piece, you'll go directly from the last note of the third line back to the first note of the first line without pausing. Keep the beat steady. In general, it's always a good idea to look through a piece before starting to play. This will give you an opportunity to find anything new or important to consider as you play. Also, it's a good idea to listen to the recording so you know how it should sound.

This is your first song using the $\frac{4}{4}$ time signature. Count four beats in every measure.

The first three notes in measure 1 are **A**'s, which are played on the open 1st string. Add your 3rd finger to the 3rd fret to play the **C** on the fourth beat. On the first beat of measure 2, place your 2nd finger on the 2nd fret to play the **B** as you lift your 3rd finger off the **C**, but keep your 3rd finger close by. After playing the **B** on the second beat, add your 3rd finger to the 3rd fret to play the **C** on the third beat, but keep your 2nd finger down on the **B**. Now, lift the 3rd finger to play the **B** on the fourth beat. Measure 3 has the same notes as measure 1, but the **C** is played on the third beat instead of the fourth. To play measure 4, place both the 2nd and 3rd fingers on the 2nd and 3rd frets, respectively. Play two **C** notes then lift the 3rd finger off to play two **B** notes, but again, keep the 3rd finger close by because measure 5 starts with returning the 3rd finger to the **C** on the 3rd fret. In measure 5, go back and forth between the C on the 3rd fret and the **A** on the open string.

Measure 6 is identical measure 2. It is always a good idea to study the music before you play to look for repeated musical ideas. Since you have already learned to play this musical pattern in measure 2, learning measure 6 will be easy.

Measure 7 starts with the **A** on the open 1st string, which is followed by by two **C**'s with the 3rd finger on the 3rd fret, and then a **B** with the 2nd finger on the 2nd fret. Measure 8 is a lot like measures 1, 3, and 5 because it includes the **A** and **C** notes, played on the open string and 3rd fret, respectively, but this time the **C** is played on the second beat.

Notice that there are two measures where you will hold down the note **B** with your 2nd finger while playing the note **C** with the 3rd finger. Can you find them? If you said the second and sixth measures, you were right!

Repeat Signs

This music uses *repeat signs*. The double dots inside the double bars tell you that everything in between those double bars is to be repeated.

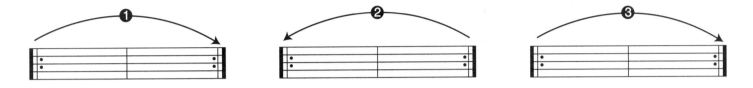

The best way to learn all the songs and exercises is to listen to the recording first so that you can hear exactly what is going to happen. Follow along in the music as you listen. Then, enjoy playing along.

1st String Blues

Track 5

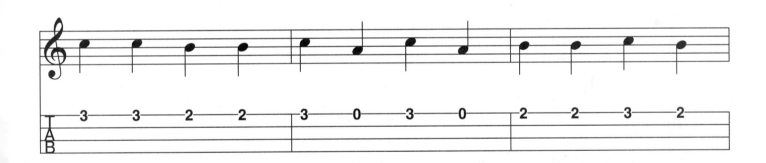

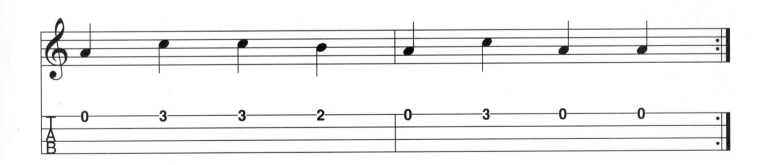

The Second String E

Now that you are comfortable playing three notes on the 1st, or **A** string, we'll be moving over to the 2nd, or **E** string and learn three more notes. Look at the top of page 23 and you will see the photos, finger diagrams, and the new notes on the music staff for the **E** string. As you hold the ukulele in playing position, the 2nd string is located one string higher (from the floor) than the 1st string, though it will sound lower in pitch. The string gets its name from the note that is sounded when it is played as an open string (not fingered).

The three notes on this string are located on the open string, 1st fret, and 3rd fret. These are **E** (the open 2nd string), **F** (the 2nd string, 1st fret), and **G** (the 2nd string, 3rd fret).

E on the 2nd String. The finger diagram on the left shows the open 2nd string **E**. Note the solid line. Pick **E** several times to hear the sound of this new string. Alternate your picking between the open 1st string **A** and the open 2nd string **E** several times. After doing this, see if you can alternate between picking the two strings without watching. **E** is located on the first line of the music staff.

F on the 2nd String. The middle diagram shows the fingering for the note **F**. It is fingered by placing your 1st finger slightly behind the 1st fret on the 2nd string. Pick **F** several times. It will sound slightly higher than the open **E**. Now raise your 1st finger slightly off the fingerboard and pick the open **E** again. Say the notes as you pick: **F, E, F, E**. The **F** is located in the first space of the staff.

G on the 2nd String. The right diagram shows the fingering for the note **G**. Place your 3rd finger slightly behind the 3rd fret on the 2nd string. Pick **G** several times. Now raise your 3rd finger slightly off the fingerboard and press your 1st finger down slightly behind the 1st fret again and pick **F**. This time, after picking **F** on the 1st fret, hold your 1st finger down as you press down your 3rd finger to pick **G**. **G** is located on the second line of the music staff.

The Pick Stroke. As mentioned before, when playing the 2nd or 3rd strings, after the pick strikes the string, let it come to rest against the next higher string. In this case, when picking the 2nd string, let the pick come to rest against the 1st string. Hold the pick firmly but without tensing the muscles of the forearm. You should feel as though the pick is "falling through" the string.

Music Exercise. Look down to the first line of music. To the left of the music staff, you will see a summary chart of the three notes and fingerings you have just learned. It is intended to be a quick review.

Begin playing the music line slowly and evenly. It is in $\frac{4}{4}$ time, so there are four beats to the measure and the quarter note receives one beat. In the 5th measure, hold your 1st finger down after picking **F** and then press down your 3rd finger for **G**, the first note in the 6th measure. Raise your 3rd finger, 3rd beat, to pick **F** in the 6th measure—your 1st finger is already down. Lift your 1st finger when picking open **E** in the 7th measure. Start slowly, and gradually increase your speed.

JAMMIN' ON TWO STRINGS

"Jammin' on Two Strings" includes all the notes on the 1st and 2nd strings you have learned so far. Quickly review the notes you learned on the 1st string before starting this piece—see the upper right corner of pg. 23 for a review of the notes on the 1st string. A good preliminary exercise would be to start on the 1st string **C** and play all the notes sequentially down to the open **E** on the 2nd string: **C–B–A–G–F–E**, saying the notes as you play. When you can accomplish this, playing smoothly and steadily with no stops, you are making excellent progress. Now, play this exercise in reverse starting on the open **E** string and going up: **E–F–G–A–B–C**, saying the notes as you play.

When you feel comfortable picking "Jammin' on Two Strings," turn the page and learn to play the next two pieces.

The Second String E Track 6

NOTES YOU'VE LEARNED SO FAR

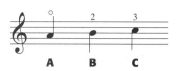

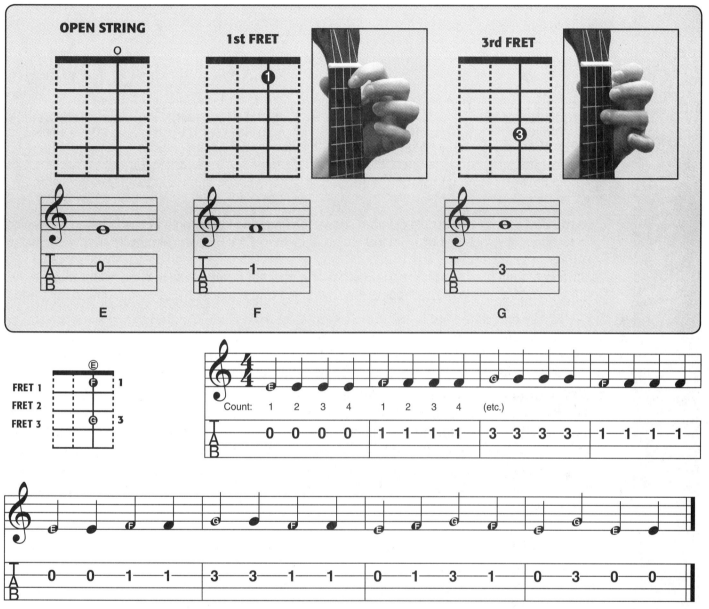

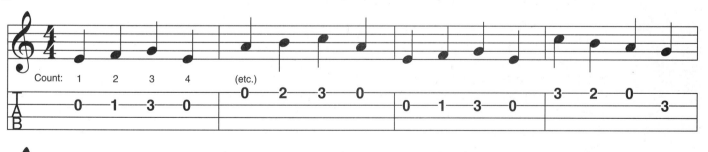

JAMMIN' ON TWO STRINGS Track 7

HOT CROSS BUNS

"Hot Cross Buns" is an English nursery rhyme. It was an Easter song, and a street cry from street vendors who sold a spiced bun associated with Good Friday.

This is your first song mixing whole, half, dotted halves, and quarter notes, here is a quick review:

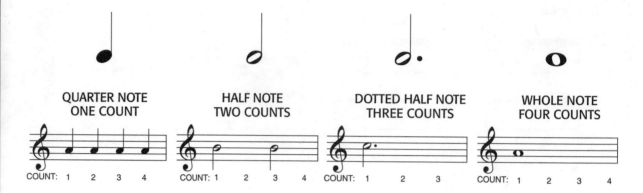

| QUARTER NOTE | HALF NOTE | DOTTED HALF NOTE | WHOLE NOTE |
| ONE COUNT | TWO COUNTS | THREE COUNTS | FOUR COUNTS |

It's always a good idea to practice the rhythm of a new song before playing it on your ukulele. Count aloud, "1–2–3–4" while clapping the rhythms. For the longer notes—half, dotted half, and whole notes—hold your hands together as you count.

When approaching a song or exercise for the first time, always look through it carefully and observe the important features. For example, "Hot Cross Buns" is in $\frac{4}{4}$ time, which means there are four counts, or beats, to a measure. Also, you will be playing some new rhythms. The first measure has two half notes, and the second measure has a whole note. The same pattern reappears in measures 3–4, 7–8, 9–10, and 11–12.

The fourth line, second measure has another new rhythm: a quarter note followed by a dotted half note ♩ ♩. You will pluck on the first and second beat, then hold the dotted half note for three beats (the remainder of the measure), counting 2–3–4. It would be a good idea to practice the first two measures of the fourth line slowly while counting aloud several times before playing the whole song.

You should have a thorough practice routine:

1. Look over every new piece first to observe all of the important features, especially new notes and rhythms.

2. Learn to count and clap the rhythms.

3. Practice saying the names of the notes aloud in rhythm as you tap your foot on every beat.

4. Practice saying the finger numbers aloud in rhythm as you tap your foot on every beat.

5. Practice playing slowly, just two measures at a time, until they feel easy to play.

Enjoy!

Hot Cross Buns

Track 8

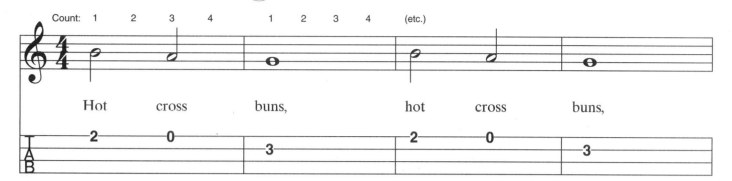

Hot cross buns, hot cross buns,

One a pen - ny, two a pen - ny, hot cross buns.

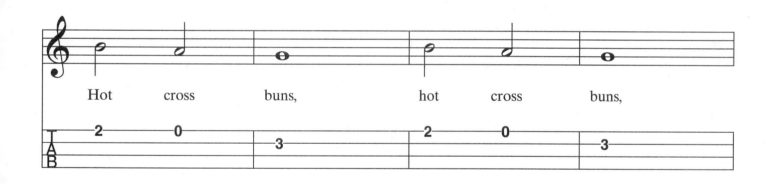

Hot cross buns, hot cross buns,

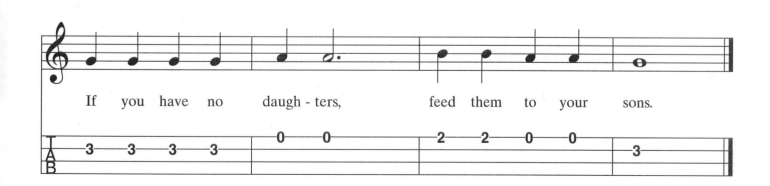

If you have no daugh - ters, feed them to your sons.

BLUES IN C

This song is played entirely on the 2nd string, with the notes **E**, **F**, and **G**. The gray characters above the music are chord symbols, and they are for a teacher or more advanced friend to play in a duet with you.

Notice that lines three and four are exactly the same as the first two lines except for the very last note. Also, notice the musical pattern that is repeated throughout—two repeated notes followed by a skip up (**G** down to **E**, skipping **F**) or skip down (**E** up to **G**, skipping **F**). Observing musical patterns such as these should be part of preparing to play any new piece of music. It makes learning and playing music easier!

Look at the rhythm of the second measure: it is quarter note–half note–quarter note (♩ ♩ ♩). You'll play on beats 1, 2, and 4, holding the second note through beat 3. This rhythm occurs three more times: in the fourth, 10th, and 12th measures.

The eighth measure also has a new rhythm: quarter note–quarter note–half note (♩ ♩ ♩). You'll play on beats 1, 2, and 3, holding the half note through beat 4.

Here are three more good tricks for making learning music easier:

1. Practice reciting the names of the notes until you can name them steadily, with ease.

2. Practice reciting the finger numbers until you can name them in a steady beat, with ease.

3. Practice playing two measures at a time, repeating them until they are easy to play. Then, do the same with the next two measures. When they feel easy to play, play all four measures. Learn two more measures, then play all six. Continue this way through the whole piece. This is called *additive practice*, and it is something you should always do when starting to learn new music.

With this in mind, here is an updated version of your practice routine:

1. Look over every new piece first to observe all of the important features, especially new notes and rhythms.

2. Learn to count and clap the rhythms.

3. Practice saying the names of the notes aloud in rhythm as you tap your foot on every beat.

4. Practice saying the finger numbers aloud in rhythm as you tap your foot on every beat.

5. Use additive practice. Practice playing slowly, just two measures at a time, until they feel easy to play. Then, do the same with the next two measures. When they feel easy to play, play all four measures. Learn two more measures, then play all six. Continue this way through the whole piece.

Most importantly, have fun!

BLUES IN C

Track 9

If the teacher wishes to play along with the student, the chord symbols above each staff may be used for a teacher-student duet. These chords are not to be played by the student.

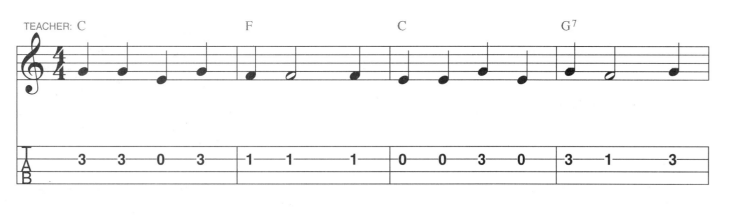

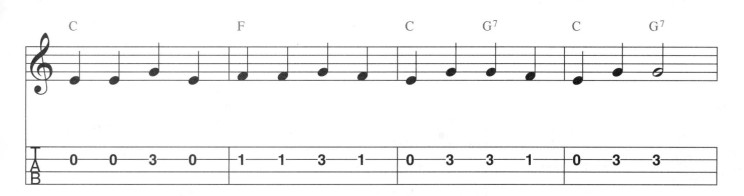

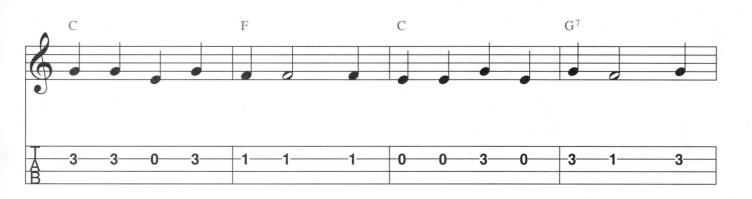

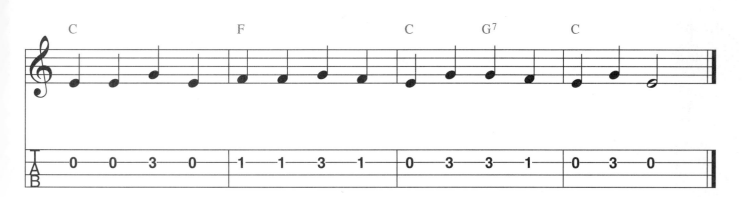

ROCKIN' UKE

"Rockin' Uke" uses notes on both the 1st and 2nd string. As with "Blues in C" on page 27, chord symbols are provided so a teacher can strum along with you.

Rock 'n' roll is a style of music that became popular in the 1950s and continues to be popular today. The roots of rock come from American blues music. The ukulele wasn't always used in rock, but it has made many appearances on recent recordings.

Notice that lines one and two have nearly identical melodies, except the fourth measures are slightly different. The same is true for lines three and four—except for the fourth measure of each line, they are identical.

The first two lines are all quarter notes. The piece is in ♩ time so you'll play on all four beats of the first eight measures. In the second eight measures, the quarter-quarter-half rhythm (♩ ♩ ♩) appears. In those measures, you'll play on beats 1, 2, and 3, holding the half note through beat 4. In the early stages with a new piece, it is a good idea to count aloud as you play. This will ensure that you understand the rhythms and are playing them accurately.

Remember to name the notes and fingers before playing, and apply additive practice (see page 26).

Always use a thorough practice routine.

1. Look over every new piece first to observe all of the important features, especially new notes and rhythms.

2. Learn to count and clap the rhythms.

3. Practice saying the names of the notes aloud in rhythm as you tap your foot on every beat.

4. Practice saying the finger numbers aloud in rhythm as you tap your foot on every beat.

5. Use additive practice. Master the first two measures, then the next two, and get comfortable with playing all four. Then practice the next two measures, and play all six, etc. This is the best, quickest way to learn a new piece.

It is a good idea to stop here, and review. Make sure you have mastered all of the pieces up to this point in the book because starting on page 30, you'll be learning a new string. Here is a quick review of the notes you have learned so far:

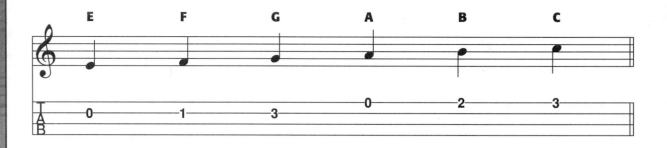

Rockin' Uke

 Track 10

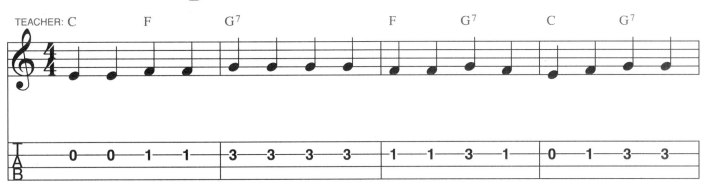

The Third String C

C on the 3rd String. Look at the top of page 31 and you will see the photo, finger diagrams, and locations on the music staff of two new notes on the **C** string. As you hold the ukulele in playing position, the 3rd string is located one string higher than the 2nd string, though it will sound lower in pitch. As you know, the string gets its name from the note that is sounded when it is played as an open string. This string is slightly thicker than the 2nd string.

Pick the 3rd string **C** several times to hear the sound of this new note. After picking the note several times and saying its letter name, pick the three open strings you now know in order from the lowest in pitch to the highest. That is 3rd string **C**, 2nd string **E**, and 1st string **A**. Say the notes as you play: **C–E–A**. Now pick the three open strings in reverse order from highest to the lowest, **A–E–C**, also saying the notes as you play.

Keep picking the strings one at a time, up and down, without stopping, saying the string names as you play. Lastly, try playing this exercise without looking at the strings. You should gradually be getting the "feel" of where the strings are located. If you can't do this right away, you will be able to very soon. **C** is located below the staff. In order to notate notes below the staff, we use temporary extensions of the staff called *ledger lines*. The word ledger is sometimes spelled *leger.* The note **C** is written on the first ledger line below the staff.

D on the 3rd String. Place your 2nd finger slightly behind the 2nd fret (see photo and finger diagram) and press down. This new note is on the 3rd string **D**. As you can see from the music staff below the finger diagram, this note is placed just below the bottom line of the staff. Since this is the first time you'll be fingering with your 2nd finger, it may take a little while to get used to the feel. Pick open string **C** then 2nd fret **D**, going back and forth between the two notes several times, saying the names of the notes, **C–D** as you play.

A good way to integrate the notes on the **C** string with the notes on the **E** string is to learn the *five–note C scale*: **C–D–E–F–G**. **C** and **D** are on the 3rd string, while **E**, **F**, and **G** are on the 2nd string. Start the exercise on low **C** and pick one higher note each time you pick until you reach **G** on the 3rd fret of the 2nd string. Then start on **G** and come down until you are back to low **C**. As always, say the names of the notes going up and down. When you can play this smoothly and evenly, you'll have no trouble with playing the tune at the bottom of the page.

The Octave. Let's talk about the differences between the higher **C** on the 1st string, 3rd fret, and the lower **C** on the open 3rd string. The two notes are said to be an *octave* apart. The word octave comes from the number *eight.* If you count up from the lower **C** (1) to the higher **C** (8), **C–D–E–F–G–A–B–C**, you'll find they are eight notes, or an *octave*, apart.

The musical notation for the two **C**'s is different, too. The lower **C** is on the first *ledger line* (a short, horizontal line which extends the staff either higher or lower) below the staff; the upper **C** is in the third space of the staff. And for all you ukulele players interested in physics, the higher **C** vibrates at exactly twice the speed of the lower **C**.

Jammin' on Three Strings

"Jammin' on Three Strings" combines the 3rd-string open **C** with notes on the 1st and 2nd strings. Notice that the melodic pattern of the first five notes is repeated in measures 3, 7, and 11. This pattern starts on low, 3rd-string **C** and moves up to the higher, 1st-string **C**. The piece is in $\frac{4}{4}$ time, and chord symbols are provided so a teacher or friend can play along.

In measure 10, hold your 1st finger down on the **F** while playing the **G** with the 3rd finger. Also, notice that measures 6 and 8 have the quarter-quarter-half rhythm (♩ ♩ ♩), and measures 4 and 12 both have two half notes. Remember to count aloud as you play.

Notice that "Jammin' on Three Strings" is 12 measures long. It uses a specific pattern of chords we call the *12-bar blues.* This is the basis for many blues, jazz, and rock songs.

The Third String C Track 11

E F G A B C

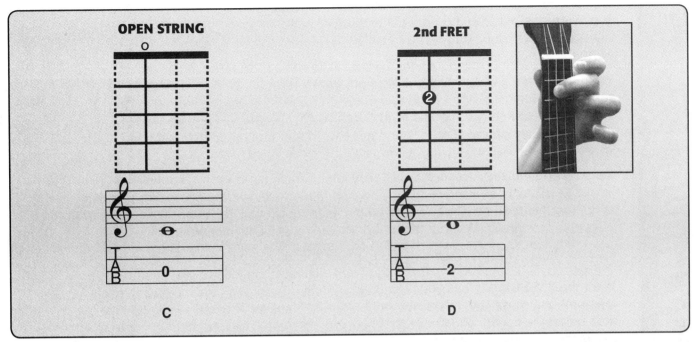

OPEN STRING

C

2nd FRET

D

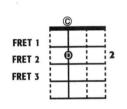

FRET 1
FRET 2
FRET 3

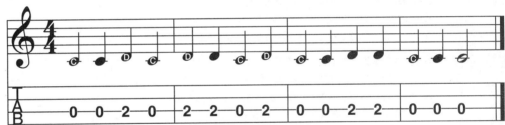

JAMMIN' ON THREE STRINGS  Track 12

LARGO

Because Italian musicians were influential in the development of music notation, especially when important advances were made in the 16th and 17th centuries, many of the music terms we use today are actually Italian words. Some of the words suggest to the musician how quickly or slowly (called *tempo* in Italian) and in what style a piece of music is to be played.

In classical music, long pieces for full orchestra are called *symphonies*. Whole sections (called *movements*) of symphonic works are sometimes referred to by their tempo indication. The famous melody on page 33 is a good example. It is popularly called *Largo*, and it is from Dvorak's *9th Symphony* (also known as *The New World Symphony*). *Largo* is an Italian word that means "at a slow tempo and in a dignified style."

When playing this type of melody, it's very important to try to keep a smooth line going. Musicians call this type of playing by another Italian word, *legato*. When a note is fingered, press down firmly and keep the finger down as long as possible until the next note is fingered. This way, the notes should be smoothly connected.

By now, you should be ready to perform music reasonably well the first time you see it. This is called *sight-reading* (reading at first sight). Do the following to improve your sight-reading skills. As *Largo* is played slowly, first look through the music and see if there are any surprises. There may not be any, but look for yourself. Only one note you know is not used, and that is **B**. When you are ready, set your metronome to a relatively slow count and begin playing. No matter what happens, keep going, even if you pick a wrong note or two. Don't expect to perform perfectly but try to come close. A piece of music is only new the first time you play it, so take a deep breath, relax, and start to play.

Tip

When playing at a slow tempo, it is easy to want to speed up. If you are working with a metronome, try hard not to play before a click. Rather, play right ON the clicks. When you play without a metronome, count every beat in your head even if you are playing a half note or whole note. In $\frac{4}{4}$ time, keep counting 1–2–3–4. If you do this, it should prevent you from speeding up.

Largo
(from the New World Symphony)

Track 13

Antonin Dvořák

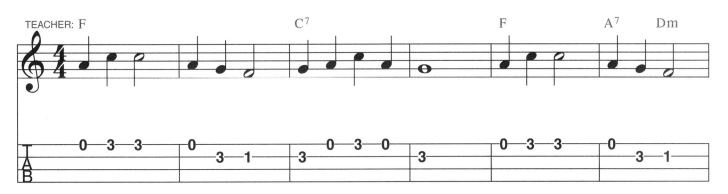

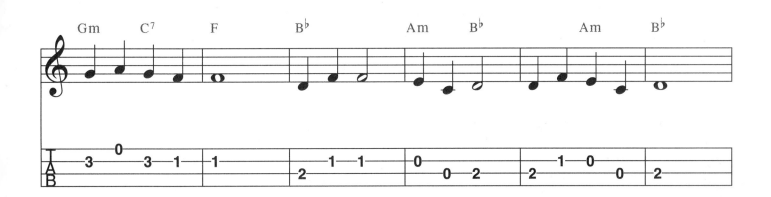

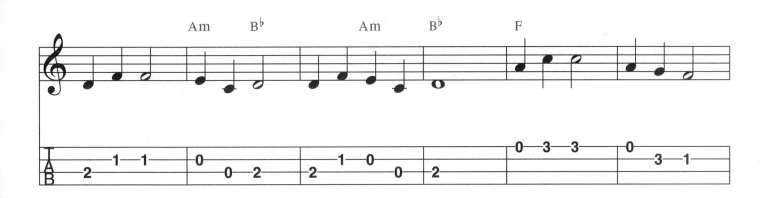

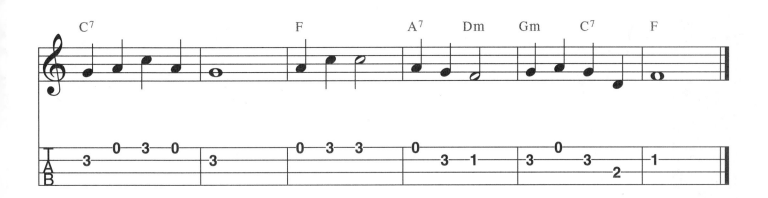

JINGLE BELLS

Composed by James Pierpont, "Jingle Bells" is probably the most popular Christmas song ever written. Pierpont wrote it for the Thanksgiving celebration of a Sunday school class, and although the lyrics never mention Christmas, the "jingle bell" rhythm proved to be irresistible and has been played and sung for that holiday for well over a hundred years.

By now, reading the notes on the music staff and picking the correct string while fingering the right fret should be almost automatic to you. Except for the octave played in the very last measure, "Jingle Bells" includes only the five notes of the five–note C scale, **C–D–E–F–G**. As a warm-up exercise, pick **C–D–E–F–G**, starting on low **C** and ending on **G**, saying the notes as you play.

Upon reaching **G**, repeat the exercise in reverse, **G–F–E–D–C**, starting on **G** and ending on **C**, saying the notes as you play.

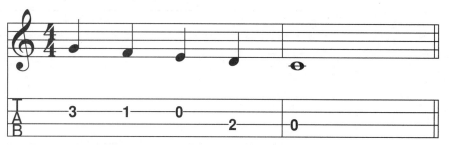

Finally, starting on **C**, pick the notes of the five–note C scale up and down without stopping, once again, saying the notes as you play: **C–D–E–F–G–F–E–D–C**. Keep playing this exercise repeatedly, up and down, picking evenly but gradually increasing your speed. The trick is to stay in control and to go only as fast as your ability allows. When you reach a comfortable speed, stop and relax your hand.

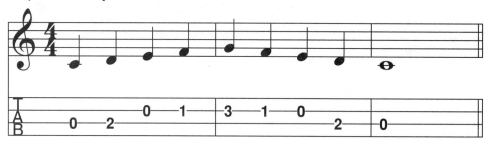

There are a few spots in the melody of "Jingle Bells" that require special attention. In measure 3, open **E** rises directly to high **G**. Go back and forth between these two notes a few times, making sure your 3rd finger presses the **E** string directly behind—not on—the 3rd fret.

In measure 7 (2nd line), open **E** on the 2nd string is followed by **D** on the 3rd string. This is a little tricky, because after playing **E** you must raise the pick back and over the 2nd and 3rd strings to be in position to pick **D** on the 3rd string. Make sure you're fingering all the fretted notes just behind the fret wires and that your sound is clear and bell-like.

If you've been counting aloud as you play, singing the lyrics of "Jingle Bells" should be easy for you. By singing and playing without looking at your hands, you are well on your way to becoming an accomplished ukulele player.

JINGLE BELLS

Track 14

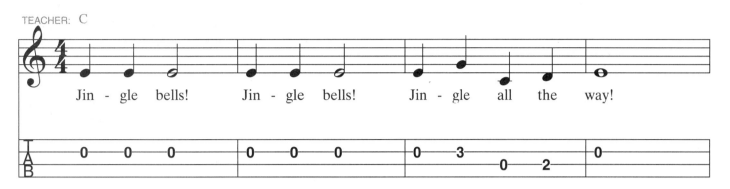

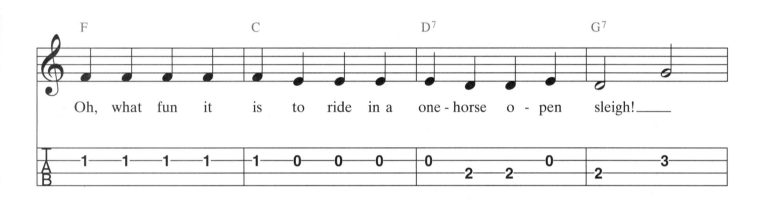

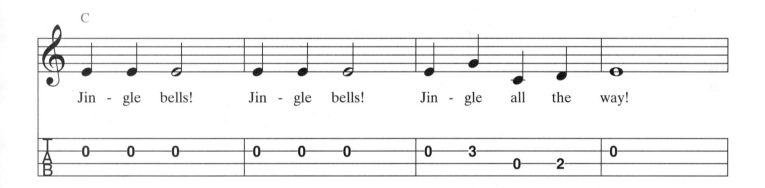

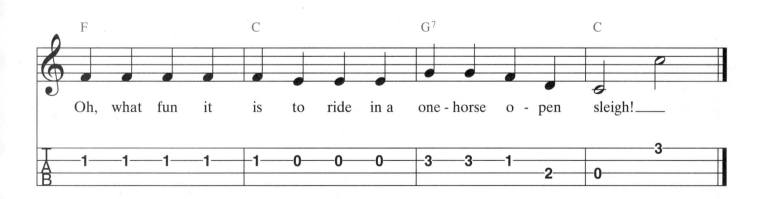

BEAUTIFUL BROWN EYES

"Beautiful Brown Eyes" became popular in the West during the 19th century. Told from a woman's perspective, it tells the story of a Mexican girl or, perhaps, an American Indian maiden, who falls in love with a cowboy who dies before they could marry.

The first, second, and third lines all start the same way, using the notes **C**, **D**, **E**, and **F**. Two of these notes, **C** and **E**, are played on open strings, and the other two, **D** and **F**, are fretted, which makes this repeated melody easy to play. The following exercise will prepare you to play the song:

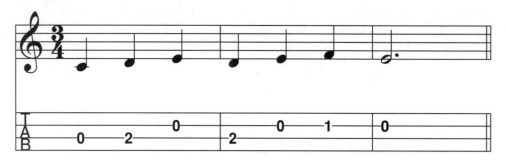

Notice that going from the end of the third line to the beginning of the fourth line requires a move from the 1st to the 3rd finger. It's always a good idea to hold the lower finger down, in this case the 1st finger, when ascending from one fretted note to another because it helps to create a smoother-sounding, legato line. If your fingers find the reach difficult in the beginning, don't worry about it. Make going from **F** to **G** an exercise and repeat it often. In time, your reach will increase.

"Beautiful Brown Eyes" is in ¾ time, so start by counting 1–2–3, then start to play.

Always use a thorough practice routine.

1. Look over every new piece first to observe all of the important features, especially new notes and rhythms.

2. Learn to count and clap the rhythms.

3. Practice saying the names of the notes aloud in rhythm as you tap your foot on every beat.

4. Practice saying the finger numbers aloud in rhythm as you tap your foot on every beat.

5. Use additive practice. Practice playing slowly, just two measures at a time, until they feel easy to play. Then, do the same with the next two measures. When those measures feel easy to play, play all four measures. Learn two more measures, then play all six. Continue this way through the whole piece.

BEAUTIFUL BROWN EYES

 Track 15

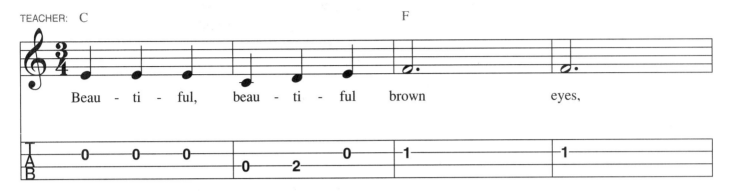

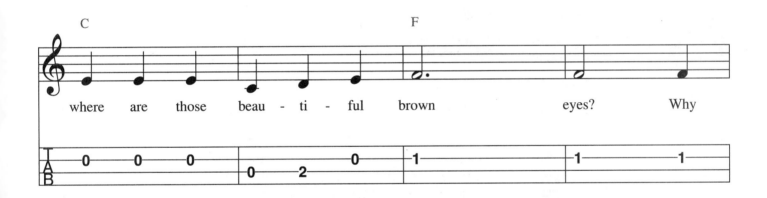

Introducing B-flat

A *flat♭* lowers a note a *half step*, which equals one fret on a ukulele. **B♭** (B-flat) is played one fret lower than the note B. Since B is played on the 2nd fret of the 1st string, **B♭** is played on the 1st fret. When a flat note appears in a measure, it is still flat until the end of that measure. Notice that, although we put the flat sign after the name of the note in text, in music notation, the sign appears directly before the note head.

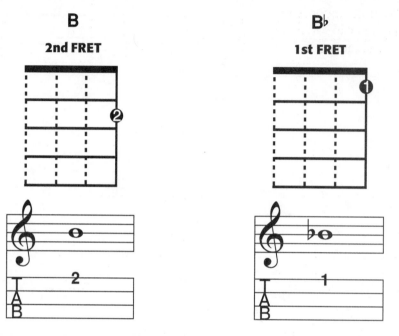

AURA LEE

This melody has an interesting history. First composed in 1861 during the Civil War with the title "Aura Lea," the song became immensely popular with soldiers from both sides of that awful war. Years later, a new set of words that spoke of the West Point Military Academy was added and the title changed to "Army Blue." Finally, in his movie debut in 1956, Elvis Presley recorded his version for a movie about the Civil War in which he acted and sang. The movie featured the song with yet another set of words and was now called "Love Me Tender." It became one of his greatest hits.

Except for the **B♭**, the notes of "Aura Lee" are notes you've played before. What is new, however, is found in the 2nd and 10th measures (both measures are the same). For the first time, you will be playing **G** (3rd finger, 2nd string), going to **D** (2nd finger, 3rd string), and then going back to **G** again. This requires some flexibility of fingers 3 and 2. Whenever you find a difficult musical passage, it is good practice to repeat that section over and over until you can perform it smoothly and easily.

Notice the repeat signs in the first line. Those four measures are played twice.

Even when you are away from the ukulele, you can practice by pressing your 3rd and 2nd fingers into the palm of your hand (as if it was the ukulele fingerboard). Gradually, the top joint of both fingers will become more flexible and playing the two measures in "Aura Lee" will no longer be a problem for you.

Since this is a romantic ballad, modify your picking to get a gentler, softer sound. Here's where you'll appreciate how important it is to press firmly behind each fret to get a lovely, bell-like sound.

Introducing B-Flat Track 16

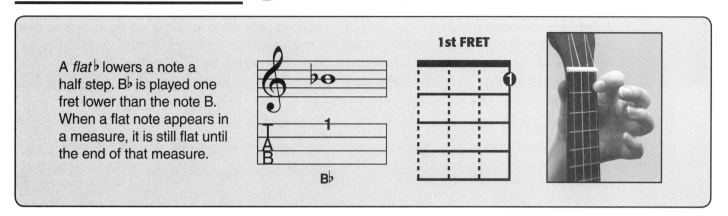

A *flat* ♭ lowers a note a half step. B♭ is played one fret lower than the note B. When a flat note appears in a measure, it is still flat until the end of that measure.

AURA LEE Track 17

This old American folk song was later recorded by Elvis Presley and called "Love Me Tender."

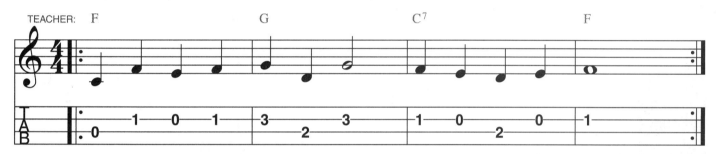

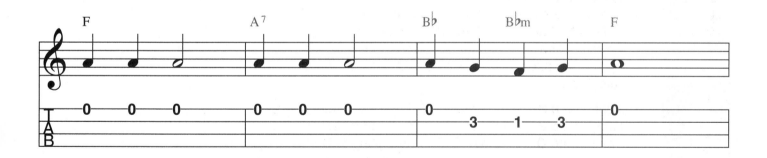

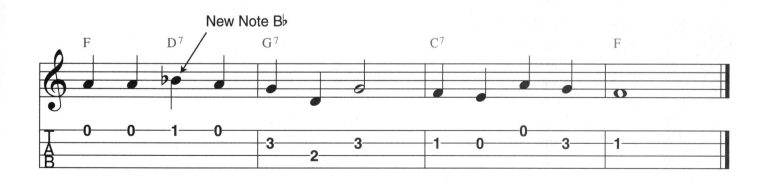

THREE-STRING BOOGIE

This fun song uses all of the notes you know, including the **B♭** you just learned. It is in ⁴⁄₄ time and chord symbols are provided so a teacher or friend can play along. Also notice the repeat signs at the beginning and end; the whole piece is played twice. "Three-String Boogie" is based on the 12-bar blues, which was introduced on pages 30.

The *boogie* style of blues became popular in the early 1900s. It started as a fast piano style with a very active left-hand part and soon was adapted for other instruments, particularly the guitar. The boogie style inspired rockabilly music and early rock 'n' roll.

You will probably find most of this tune easy to sight-read. It will not take you long to learn. The only tricky spot is in measure 9 at the end of the third line. You'll need to move from **G** on the 3rd fret of the 2nd string to **D** on the 2nd fret of the 3rd string, then move the 2nd finger directly across to **B** (not **B♭**!) on the 2nd fret of the 1st string. This will require the finger to "hop" over the 2nd string as it moves from the 3rd string to the 1st string. When you lift the 2nd finger from the 3rd string, move it directly down toward the 1st string. Avoid lifting it up, away from the fret, before moving toward the 1st string. Move directly, smoothly, and with as little energy as possible. The finger should make just a smooth little hop, not a big, jerky jump.

This exercise will help prepare you for this move. Play it slowly, over and over, until it is easy. Master it before attempting to sight-read "Three-String Boogie."

Notice the repeat marks at the beginning and end of the piece. Be sure to play it twice!

Always use a thorough practice routine.

1. Look over every new piece first to observe all of the important features, especially new notes and rhythms.

2. Learn to count and clap the rhythms.

3. Practice saying the names of the notes aloud in rhythm as you tap your foot on every beat.

4. Practice saying the finger numbers aloud in rhythm as you tap your foot on every beat.

5. Use additive practice. Practice playing slowly, just two measures at a time until they feel easy to play. Then, do the same with the next two measures. When those two measures feel easy to play, play all four measures. Learn two more measures, then play all six. Continue this way through the whole piece.

THREE-STRING BOOGIE Track 18

This song uses all the notes you have learned. Don't forget to listen to the audio on the CD or DVD first!

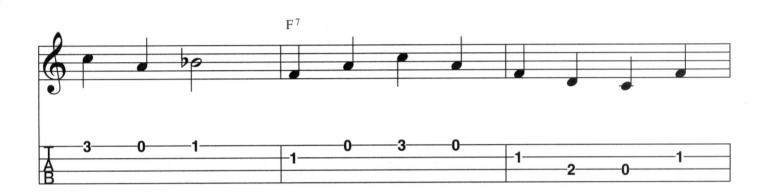

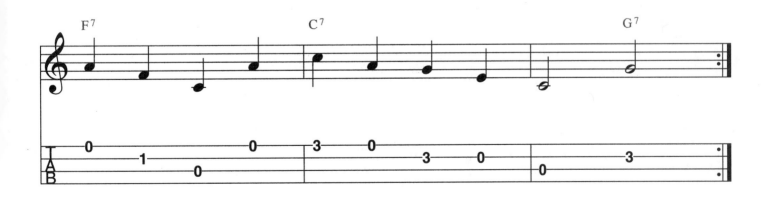

Tempo Signs

Around the year 1600, musicians in Europe began to standardize music notation. This included the notes themselves as well as other signs used on the music page. As mentioned earlier, Italian musicians were predominant, so many of the musical symbols and words we still use are of Italian origin.

The word *tempo* itself is an Italian word that means time. We still use it to mean the speed at which a piece is played. Other words specifically tell us how fast or how slow a piece is to be played.

Andante (pronounced: ahn-DAHN-tay) is translated on page 43 as *slow*. Another translation might be *at a walking pace.* In any case, unlike a metronome marking which is exact, andante is not an exact speed but varies with the player's ability, taste, and even mood. Andante is definitely slower than the two tempo indications discussed next.

Moderato (moh-deh-RAH-toh) is faster than andante and is usually played at approximately 96 beats per minute, or so. It's a good idea to own a *metronome*, which is an adjustable device that can measure beats per minute and produce an audible clicking sound at the desired tempo. But as we mentioned above, these tempo indications are not exact and should be taken as suggestions only.

Allegro (ah-LAY-groh) is not only faster than moderato, but the word in Italian implies a happy, joyous feeling. As a guideline, you can set your metronome to 120 beats per minute—but don't forget that this is only a suggestion.

Quarter Rest

On page 43 you will see a somewhat odd-looking symbol called a *quarter rest*. In $\frac{4}{4}$ and $\frac{3}{4}$ time, it represents one beat of silence. It is important to remember that this is a *measured* silence, and that the basic beat of the music continues throughout. To stop the sound from the previous note or chord, you may bend your right wrist so the side (or heel) of your right hand touches the string or strings to stop the sound. Just remember to maintain a steady beat and that the next note or chord begins on the next beat.

THREE-TEMPO ROCKIN' UKE

This is another version of the 12-bar blues progression. It uses notes on the 1st, 2nd, and 3rd strings, and includes the **B**♭ note. This would have been a typical ukulele part in the early days of rock. Play it with a strong, driving beat.

"Three-Tempo Rockin' Uke" is to be played three times. The first time, the tempo is andante, or slow. Then, play this rock piece at a faster tempo, moderato, or moderately. Lastly, repeat the piece once again, playing it in an allegro tempo, or fast. To sum up, play "Three-Tempo Rockin' Uke" three times, starting slowly and each time playing it a little faster. How fast? As we said above, that's up to you.

Tempo Signs

A *tempo sign* tells you how fast to play the music. Below are the three most common tempo signs, which are Italian words. In some music, you will see tempo signs written in English.

Andante ("ahn-DAHN-teh") means to play slow.

Moderato ("moh-deh-RAH-toh") means to play moderately.

Allegro ("ah-LAY-groh") means to play fast.

Quarter Rest

This sign indicates silence for one count. For a clearer effect, you may stop the sound of the strings by touching the strings lightly with the heel of the right hand.

THREE-TEMPO ROCKIN' UKE   Track 19

Play three times: first time **Andante**, second time **Moderato**, third time **Allegro**.

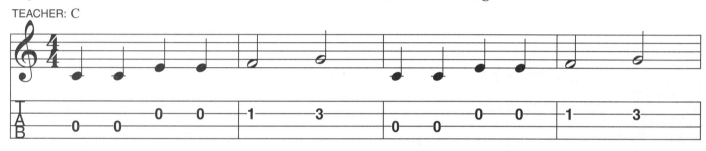

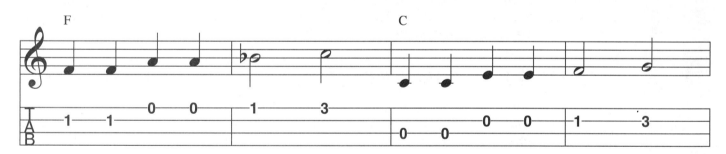

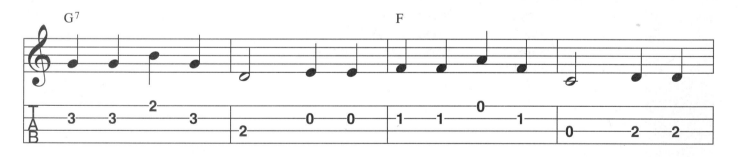

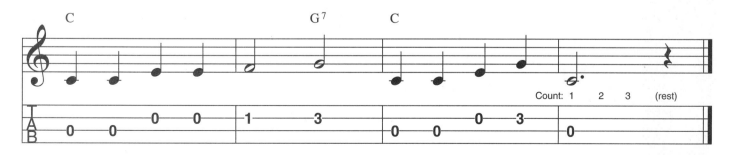

Introducing Chords

Now that you can play notes on three strings, you are ready to begin playing one of the most wonderful things about the ukulele and that is *chords.* A chord is a group of three or more notes played either simultaneously or one at a time.

On a keyboard, you can press down three or more keys at the same time to produce a chord. On a ukulele, however, the strings must be *strummed* so quickly—with a rapid stroke of the pick—so that they will sound as if they were picked simultaneously.

One way to notate chords is with *chord diagrams*, which graphically show how chords are played. Each of the vertical lines represents a string. If the string is shown as a dotted line, don't strum it with the chord. If it is to played open, a small o will be shown above the string. Fretted notes are shown with black notes with finger numbers.

Chord Diagrams

Chord diagrams are used to indicate fingering for chords. The example here means to place your 1st finger on the 1st fret, 1st string, then strum all four strings. The o symbols on the 2nd, 3rd, and 4th strings indicate to play them open (not fingered).

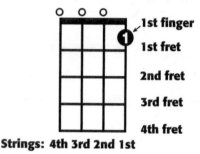

The C7 Chord

C7 is an easy chord because it requires only one left-hand finger on the 1st fret of the 1st string. Look at the chord diagram and photograph on page 45.

Examples 1, 2, and 3 at the bottom of the page should be strummed slowly with an even beat. The first one is in $\frac{2}{4}$ and has two counts, or strums, per measure. The second is in $\frac{3}{4}$ and the fourth is in $\frac{4}{4}$. Strum every time you see either a chord symbol (C7) or a slash (╱). Below is a review of all three time signatures.

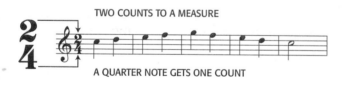

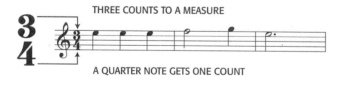

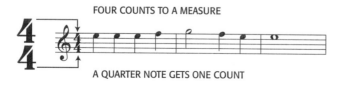

The C7 Chord Track 20

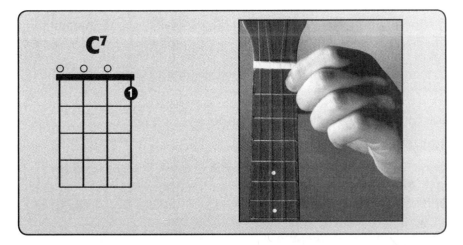

o = open string

----- = string is not played

Place your 1st finger in position, then play one string at a time.

Play all four strings
together:

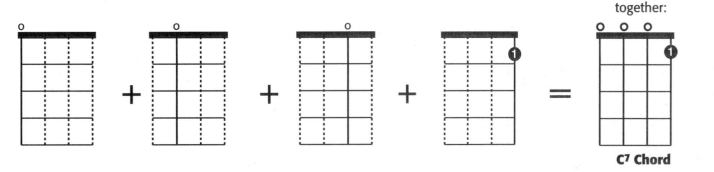

C⁷ Chord

Track 21

Play slowly and evenly. Each slash mark ⁄ means to repeat the previous chord. Strum downward for each chord name and slash mark. Use your finger or a pick. The chord name is repeated in each measure.

The F Chord

The F chord is the first chord you will play that involves fingering on the 4th string and the use of two fingers of your left hand. As the chord diagram and photo on page 47 show, you'll place your 2nd finger on the 2nd fret of the 4th string and your 1st finger on the 1st fret of the 2nd string. Be careful not to bump the open 3rd or 1st strings with your fretting fingers. You want all four strings to ring clearly. Make sure you're using the very tips of your fingers and that you curl your finger joints. With your thumb placed behind the neck, this will enable you to touch just the intended strings with your fretting fingers. Remember to place the fingertips just to the left of the frets and not directly on them.

The first three examples on page 47 are just like the C7 examples on page 45 but use an F chord instead. The bottom three examples combine the C7 and F chords. As a warm-up, place your fingers on the F chord and strum. Then, release the 2nd finger from the 4th string and smoothly move your 1st finger across to the 1st fret of the 1st string and strum the C7 chord. Be sure to keep your 2nd finger poised above the strings as you play C7 so you can easily return the fingers to the F chord. Switch back and forth between the two chords until you can easily get from one to the other with confidence.

Your finger movements should be small and smooth. Do not squeeze your ukulele. Never press harder than is absolutely necessary to make the notes ring clearly. It's about accuracy and good finger placement, not strength. Your goal is for the chords to feel easy to play. You should never press so hard that you feel any pain. The tips of your fingers may feel a little discomfort before they have developed calluses, but you should not feel any pain in your fingers, hand, wrist, arm, neck, or back from playing ukulele. If you do start to experience pain, an expert instructor may be able to help. You may also want to discuss it with a physician.

In the final three exercises on page 47, notice that you strum the final F chord in Example 1 (in $\frac{4}{4}$) only once, then hold it for the second, third, and fourth beats. In Example 2 ($\frac{3}{4}$), be silent for the quarter rests on beats 2 and 3 of the last measure by stopping the strings from vibrating with the side of your right hand. In Example 3 ($\frac{2}{4}$), strum on every beat.

The F Chord Track 22

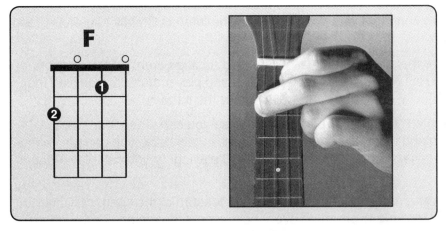

**ANOTHER CHORD
ON THIS PAGE**

C^7

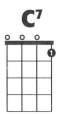

Place your 1st and 2nd fingers in position, then play one string at a time.

Play all four strings
together:

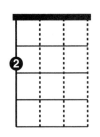 + 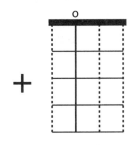 + 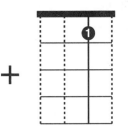 + 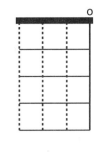 =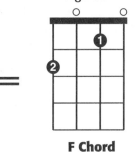

F Chord

 Track 23

1. $\begin{array}{c}2\\4\end{array}$ F / | F / | F / | F / | F / | F / ||

2. $\begin{array}{c}3\\4\end{array}$ F / / | F / / | F / / | F / / ||

3. $\begin{array}{c}4\\4\end{array}$ F / / / | F / / / | F / / / ||

 Track 24

Once you can play both the F and C7 chords clearly, try combining them as in the
following exercises.

1. $\begin{array}{c}4\\4\end{array}$ F / / / | F / / / | C7 / / / | C7 / / / | F / / / | C7 / / / | F / / / | F ||
HOLD

2. $\begin{array}{c}3\\4\end{array}$ F / / | F / / | C7 / / | C7 / / | F / / | C7 / / | F / / | F 𝄼 𝄼 ||
COUNT: 1 REST REST

3. $\begin{array}{c}2\\4\end{array}$ F / | F / | C7 / | C7 / | F / | C7 / | F / | F / ||

GOOD NIGHT LADIES

This song is actually two songs in one. The first eight measures features the melody for "Good Night, Ladies," a minstrel show song that was popularized by the famous Christy Minstrels group in the middle of the 19th century.

The last eight measures share the same melody as "Mary Had a Little Lamb." In this version, the tune is called "Merrily We Roll Along." In the late 1860s, some clever musician realized that the two songs fit together perfectly—and that's the way we play them today.

This arrangement uses both the F and the C7 chords. It's in $\frac{4}{4}$ so you can strum four times in every measure. For this song and most of the rest of the songs in this book, you can play either the melody or chords. Your teacher can play the part you aren't playing, or you can play along with the recording.

If there is no chord symbol over a measure, as in the second measure of the song, continue to play the last chord indicated. Continue to strum on every beat even if the melody has a longer note, such as a half note, dotted half note, or whole note. In measure 7, there are two chords. Play the F chord on beats 1 and 2, and the C7 on beats 3 and 4. Notice there is a quarter rest on the fourth beat of the very last measure.

Notice the tempo is moderato. Play neither quickly nor slowly. When playing the melody, pay special attention to the quarter, dotted-half-note rhythm ♩ ♩.. Play on beats 1 and 2, holding for beats 3 and 4. Also, make sure you're comfortable with the quarter–half–quarter rhythm (♩ ♩ ♩) in measure 6. Play on beats 1 and 2, holding through beat 3, then play on beat 4.

Study Guide

GOOD NIGHT LADIES

Track 25 Melody & Chords **Track 26** Chords Only

CHORDS USED IN THIS SONG

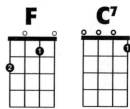

For this song and most of the rest of the songs in this book, you can play either the melody or chords. Your teacher can play the part you aren't playing, or you can play along with the CD or DVD.

Moderato

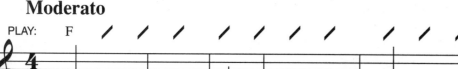

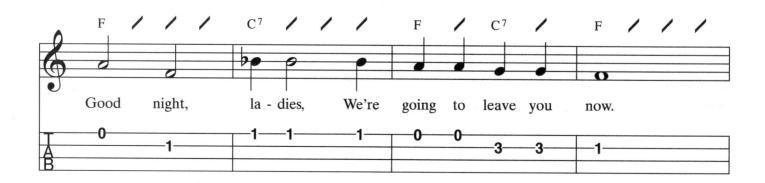

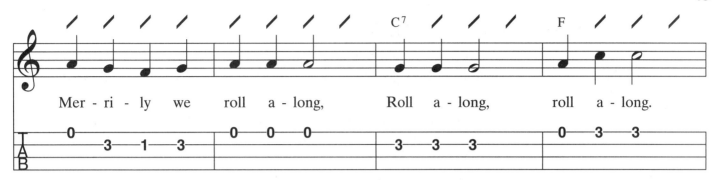

Mer - ri - ly we roll a - long, Roll a - long, roll a - long.

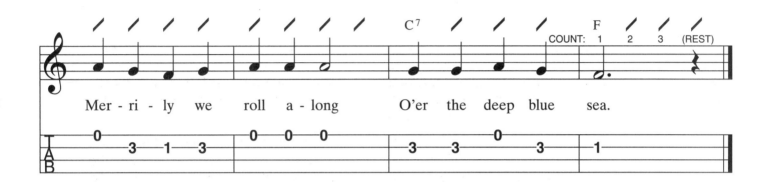

Mer - ri - ly we roll a - long O'er the deep blue sea.

COUNT: 1 2 3 (REST)

Key Signatures

Key Signature

The *key signature* just to the right of the clef at the beginning of a piece tells you when a note is played as a flat note throughout the piece. In "Down in the Valley" on page 50, each **B** is played as **B♭**.

Ties

A *tie* is a curved line that connects two notes of the same pitch. The value of the second note is tied to that of the first. For example, when a dotted half note **E**, which equals three beats, is tied to a second dotted half note **E**, the end result is an **E** note that lasts six beats.

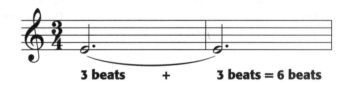

3 beats + 3 beats = 6 beats

DOWN IN THE VALLEY

"Down in the Valley" on pages 50–51 uses a key signature, ties, and notes on the 1st, 2nd, and 3rd strings. Because the time signature is ¾, you'll find lots of dotted half notes, which last for three beats.

Notice that in the ukulele tablature, a note that is being held in a tie is shown in parentheses.

Study Guide

Key Signatures

The *key signature* at the beginning of a piece tells you when a note is played as a flat note throughout the piece. In "Down in the Valley," each B is played as B-flat.

Ties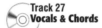

This curved line is called a *tie*. It connects two or more notes and ties them together. Play or sing the note once and hold it for the value of both (or more) tied notes.
In TAB, a tied note is shown as a number in parentheses. Do not pick the note again.

CHORDS USED IN THIS SONG

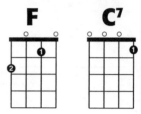

DOWN IN THE VALLEY

Track 27 Vocals & Chords   Track 28 Chords Only

Key signature: remember to play each B one half step lower.

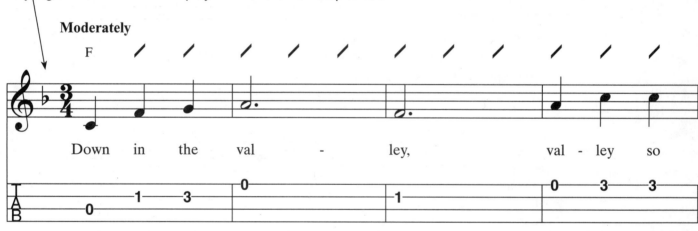

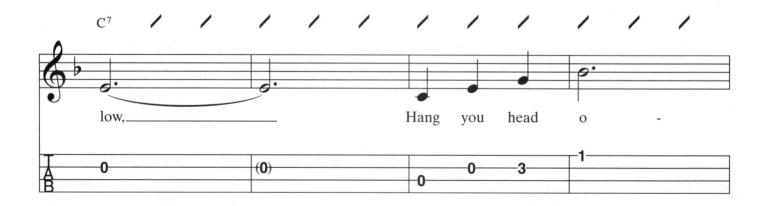

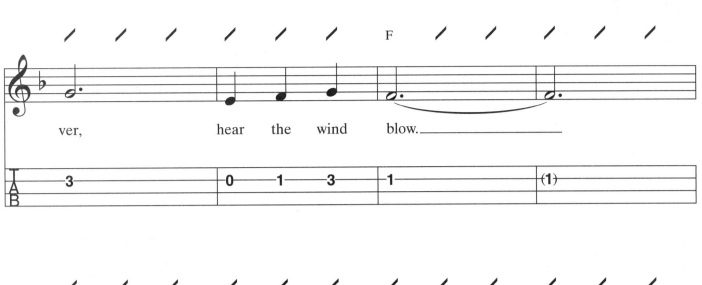

ver,   hear   the   wind   blow._____

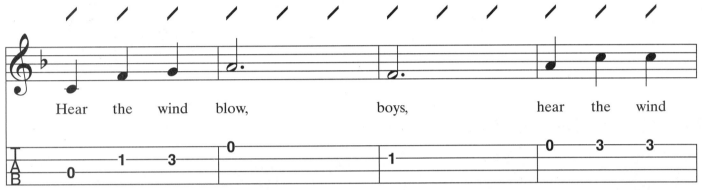

Hear   the   wind   blow,   boys,   hear   the   wind

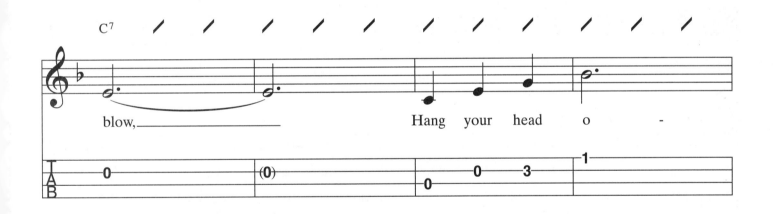

blow,_____   Hang   your   head   o   -

COUNT: 1   (2)   (3)
            (REST) (REST)

ver,   hear   the   wind   blow._____

ODE TO JOY

Like "Largo" (page 33), "Ode to Joy" is a melody from a symphony. This famous melody was composed for the final movement of Ludwig van Beethoven's monumental *Symphony No. 9*. Miraculously, Beethoven was completely deaf when he composed it in 1824.

"Ode to Joy" is in $\frac{4}{4}$ time and has a **B♭** in the key signature. You can play either the melody or the chords. The melody is fairly easy to play because it only uses the notes **F**, **G**, **A**, **B♭**, and **C** (both high and low). When ascending from **B♭** to **C** on the 1st string (as in the first measure), or from **F** to **G** on the 2nd string (as in the third measure), hold your 1st finger down on its note while you play the next note with your 3rd finger. You should be accustomed to this stretch by now.

As you are looking over the piece, notice that the first, second, and fourth lines start the same but end differently. The second and fourth lines are exactly the same except for the very last note of the fourth line, which is a quarter note and quarter rest instead of a half note. Noticing this kind of similarity makes it much easier to learn a new piece.

This arrangement also uses the F and C7 chords. In measures 8–12, the chords change every two beats, so you will want to make sure you are very comfortable with switching between the two chords.

Have fun playing this classical masterpiece!

As always, use a thorough practice routine.

1. Look over every new piece first to observe all of the important features, especially repeated musical ideas, new notes, and rhythms.

2. Learn to count and clap the rhythms.

3. Practice saying the names of the notes aloud in rhythm as you tap your foot on every beat.

4. Practice saying the finger numbers aloud in rhythm as you tap your foot on every beat.

5. Use additive practice. Practice playing slowly, just two measures at a time until they feel easy to play. Then, do the same with the next two measures. When those feel easy to play, play all four measures. Learn two more measures, then play all six. Continue this way through the whole piece.

Self-Teaching Study Guide

ODE TO JOY

Track 29
Melody & Chords

Track 30
Chords Only

Theme from Beethoven's *Symphony No. 9*

Moderato

The C Chord

It's time for a new chord! The C chord is easy to play. It's very similar to playing the **C** note: place your 3rd finger at the 3rd fret of the 1st string but instead of picking just the 1st string, strum all four. Look at the chord diagram and photograph at the top of page 55.

The first three examples in the middle of page 55 will give you practice playing the C chord in $\frac{2}{4}$, $\frac{3}{4}$, and $\frac{4}{4}$ time. The next three examples, at the bottom of the page, combine all three chords you know: C, C7, and F. Practice each one slowly until they're easy to play, then try them a bit faster. Try to visualize (get a mental picture of) your finger(s) on the next chord before you move to it, and make your movements small and smooth. Your fingers should never move in a jerky, stiff manner. Remember to press just firmly enough, directly next to the frets; don't squeeze the ukulele.

When changing from one chord to another, release the tension from the finger(s) holding the notes of the first chord but remain close to the strings. Then gently, smoothly, and directly move to the next chord, and then add only so much pressure to the string as is necessary to make the new chord sound clearly when you strum the strings. Do not press too hard. Strive to make your finger action smooth, graceful, and accurate. Think about professional musicians you have seen playing. They make it look easy, don't they? Well…it is! They practice a lot to make it easy. And it's very important to remember that ease comes from practicing ease. Practicing difficulty will not lead to ease. Find a tempo (speed) at which you can play with ease. If you repeat something enough with a feeling of ease, you will eventually be able to play it more quickly, easily.

Here is an exercise to help improve your accuracy when changing between the chords. Play this slowly. During the quarter rests, slowly lift your fingers off the strings (but staying close to the strings) and slowly but directly move to the next chord. When placing fingers for the F chord, which has two fingers, work on placing both fingers on their respective frets and strings at exactly the same time, gently.

Repeat. Start slowly, and speed up as ease and confidence increase.

The C Chord

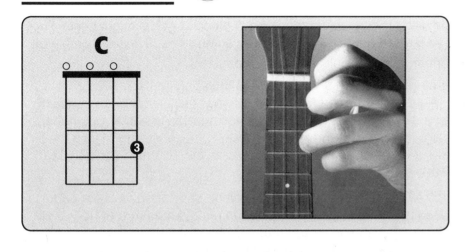

OTHER CHORDS ON THIS PAGE

Place your 3rd finger in position, then play one string at a time.

Play all four strings together:

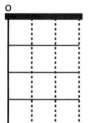 + 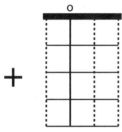 + 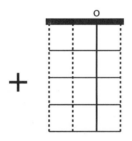 + 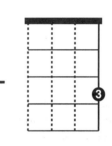 =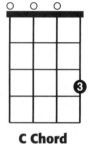

C Chord

Play slowly and evenly.

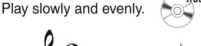

1.

2.

3.

Now try these exercises. They combine all the chords you know.

1.

2.

3.

Incomplete Measures

Music pieces sometimes begin with an *incomplete measure.* A piece in $\frac{4}{4}$ time might begin with a measure that contains only three beats, two beats, or even one beat. These incomplete measures are also called *upbeats,* or *pickups.*

Why do we need pickups? It's all because of the accents. Take the song on page 57, for example. The first words are, "A-tisket, a-tasket, I found a yellow basket." If you listen carefully as you say the first few words, you'll notice that the first accented syllable is not "A" but, rather, "tis." Since we know the first note in each measure gets an accent, it's necessary to sing the "A" before the first beat of the measure so that the syllable "tis" falls on the accented (or first) beat. That is why we have a one-beat pickup.

Often, if a song has a pickup, the last measure of the song will be shortened to make up for the omitted beats in the first incomplete measure. Because the pickup measure of "A-Tisket, A-Tasket" has only one beat (a quarter note), the last measure has only three beats (a half note and a quarter note). The total beats of the two incomplete measures is four, the correct total for one measure of $\frac{4}{4}$ time.

Below is an example of incomplete measures in $\frac{3}{4}$ time. Notice there is a quarter note pickup, so the last measure has only two beats.

A-Tisket, A-Tasket

This very old nursery rhyme is a good example of a song that requires a one-beat pickup. Count 1–2–3 and start playing on 4. Notice that the tempo is allegro, so practice it until you can play it at a lively, somewhat-quick pace.

Here is a helpful fingering hint for the fifth and sixth measures. (The pickup measure is not counted as a measure.) In the fifth measure, keep your 1st finger down on F on the 1st fret of the 2nd string while playing the D with your 2nd finger on the 2nd fret of the 3rd string. Then keep both fingers down because they are both repeated in the next measure. Easy!

Self-Teaching Study Guide

Incomplete Measures

Not all pieces of music begin on the first beat. Sometimes, music begins with an incomplete measure called a *pickup.* If the pickup is one beat, often the last measure will only have three beats in $\frac{4}{4}$, or two beats in $\frac{3}{4}$.

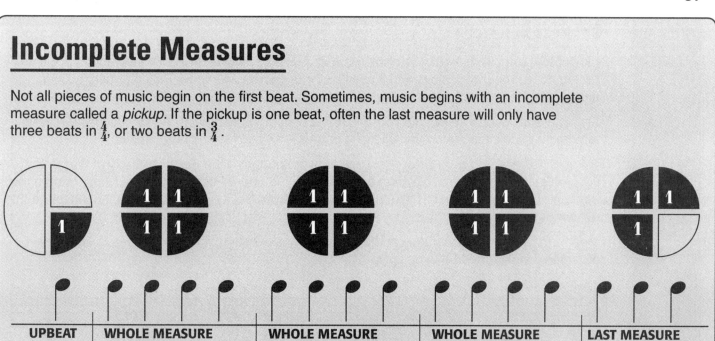

UPBEAT	WHOLE MEASURE	WHOLE MEASURE	WHOLE MEASURE	LAST MEASURE
4	1 2 3 4	1 2 3 4	1 2 3 4	1 2 3

CHORDS USED IN THIS SONG

F   C   C⁷

A-TISKET, A-TASKET

Track 34 Melody & Chords   Track 35 Chords Only

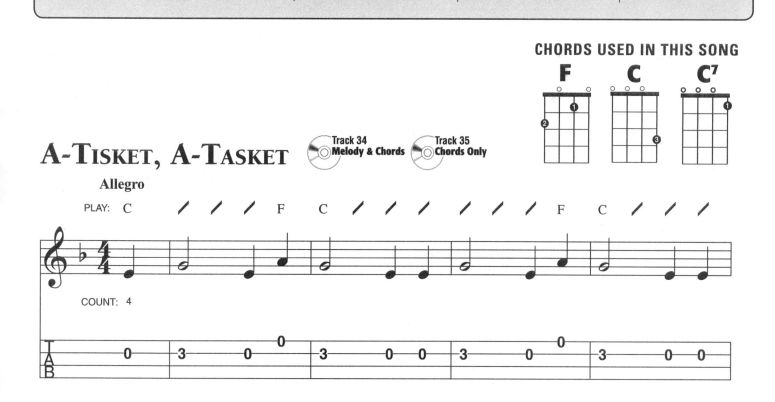

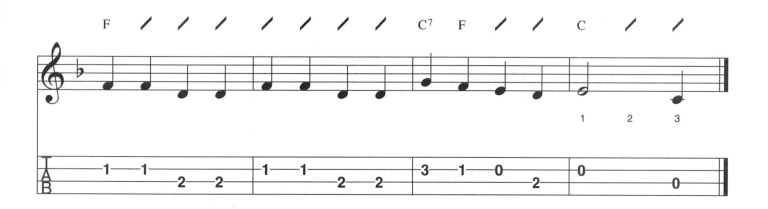

TOM DOOLEY

This old folk song from North Carolina has a **B♭** in the key signature, uses ties, and is in $\frac{4}{4}$ time. The tempo is moderately slow, and it uses all three chords you know. Play the melody, then enjoy playing the chords and singing the words.

This is an easy song to play, and you will probably find you can sight-read it successfully. Enjoy the relaxed pace because on the following pages, we'll start speeding things up.

This song is based on a true story of a soldier who fought for the South in the Civil War. After Tom Dooley returned home following the war, he killed Laura Foster. The tragic story caught the attention of people outside of Tom's hometown of Happy Valley, North Carolina, and inspired this now-famous song.

To perform the rhythm accurately in this moderately slow song, it is a good idea to keep the count going in your head as you play.

As always, use a thorough practice routine.

1. Look over every new piece first to observe all of the important features, especially repeated musical ideas, new notes, and rhythms.

2. Learn to count and clap the rhythms.

3. Practice saying the names of the notes aloud in rhythm as you tap your foot on every beat.

4. Practice saying the finger numbers aloud in rhythm as you tap your foot on every beat.

5. Use additive practice. Practice playing slowly, just two measures at a time until they feel easy to play. Then, do the same with the next two measures. When those measures feel easy to play, play all four measures. Learn two more measures, then play all six. Continue this way through the whole piece.

Have fun!

TOM DOOLEY

Track 36 Vocals & Chords   Track 37 Chords Only

CHORDS USED IN THIS SONG

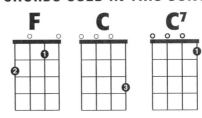

Moderately slow

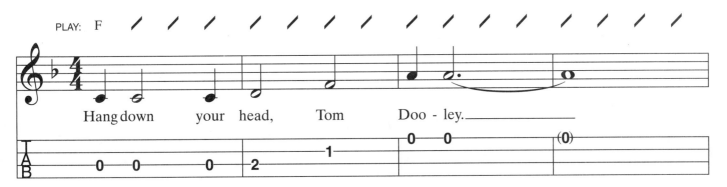

Hang down your head, Tom Doo - ley.

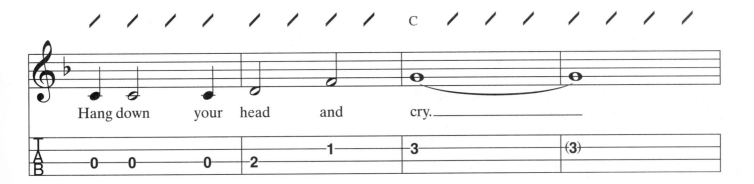

Hang down your head and cry.

Hang down your head, Tom Doo - ley.

Poor boy, you're bound to die.

Eighth Notes

Up till now in this book, we have shown you how to play notes that last one beat or longer. We will now discuss how to subdivide the beat into notes that are shorter than one beat. Try this: tap your foot and say *ta* for each time your foot goes *down.* As you've learned, you're singing quarter notes—one for each beat. Now, also say *ta* for each time your foot comes *up,* adding these to the other *ta's* you've been saying. You'll be saying a *ta* for each time your foot goes *down* as well as each time it comes *up.* Thinking in $\frac{4}{4}$ time, this means you'll be saying eight *ta's* per measure. These are called—logically enough—*eighth notes.*

Pick up your ukulele and try the same thing on any open string. First, play a *down-pick* on each downbeat. Count 1–2–3–4. Now, also play an *up-pick* on each upbeat. Count by saying, 1 and, 2 and–3 and–4 and. Or, to put it in shorter form: 1 &–2 &–3 &–4 &. Since you haven't played up-picks before, let's talk about them a bit.

You already know about letting your down-picks come to rest on the next higher string. The symbol for a down-pick is ⊓. The symbol for an up-pick is ∨. After an up-pick, you'll be floating above the string you just played. Don't let your pick stroke be too wide. You should stop the pick just a short way past the picked string, certainly no more than a quarter of an inch.

Before even attempting any of the material on page 61, try playing a series of eighth notes (down-picks and up-picks) on any open string until you can do this smoothly and evenly. After this, make an exercise out of the second measure of "Jammin' with Eighth Notes" (bottom of page 61). This will be an exercise in playing fingered notes in eighth notes with down-picks and up-picks. Repeat this exercise (measure 2) several times. Important: this technique, called *alternate picking,* is the very basis for playing with good speed and accuracy on the ukulele. You should devote a few minutes to it at every practice session.

JAMMIN' WITH EIGHTH NOTES

If you followed the suggestion above, you have already practiced the second measure of this rock tune. Notice that measures 2, 4, and 6 have exactly the same notes as the measures they follow; you're just picking eighth notes instead of quarter notes.

When strumming the chords, stay with quarter-note strums. Strumming eighth notes against eighth notes in the melody would sound very busy.

Eighth Notes Track 38

Eighth notes are black notes with a flag added to the stem: ♪ or ♩ .

Two or more eighth notes are written with beams: ♫ or ♫ , ♬ or ♬ .

Each eighth note receives one half beat.

WHOLE NOTE		2 HALF NOTES		4 QUARTER NOTES		8 EIGHTH NOTES

Use alternating down-strokes ⊓ and up-strokes ∨ on eighth notes.

COUNT: 1 & 2 & 3 & 4 & 1 & 2 & 3 & 4 &

CHORDS USED IN THIS SONG

C   C⁷   F

JAMMIN' WITH EIGHTH NOTES

Track 39 — Melody & Chords   Track 40 — Chords Only

Allegro moderato*

PLAY: C / / /   C⁷ / / /   F / / /   / / /

COUNT: 1 2 3 4   1 & 2 & 3 & 4 &   (etc.)

C / / /   C⁷ / / /   F / / /   C / / /

Allegro moderato means moderately fast.

GO TELL AUNT RHODY

This old American folk song has a **B♭** in the key signature, uses eighth notes with alternate picking, and is in ¼ time. The tempo is moderato, and it uses the F and C7 chords. Play the melody, then enjoy playing the chords and singing the words.

Notice that the eighth notes are in measure 6. The notes fall on 4 &. The trick is to start counting eighth notes, 1 &–2 &–3 & at the beginning of the measure. The measure starts with a half note and a quarter note, so play on 1 and 3 while counting the eighth notes. This will prepare you to play eighth notes on 4 &. This technique is called *preparatory counting*. It is a great practice habit to get into. Try it!

Dotted Quarter Notes (PAGE 64)

Remember, placing a dot after a note adds half its value to the original note (page 18). As an example, a *half note* is held for two beats, or counts. But when you add a dot after the half note, it adds one beat (half of two), which is the value of a *quarter note*. The *dotted half note,* then, is held for a total of three beats. It is as though we tied a quarter note to the original half note. See the first music example at the top of page 64.

The situation is similar for *dotted quarter notes.* A quarter note is held for one beat, or count. But when you add a dot after the quarter note, it adds a half beat (half of one), which is the value of an *eighth note.* The dotted quarter note, then, is held for a total of one and a half beats. It is as though we tied an eighth note to a quarter note. See the second music example at the top of page 64.

Preparatory Drill (PAGE 64)

Look at the first measure of "Preparatory Drill." It is counted as you have previously, with the *quarter note* held for one beat and the two *eighth notes* held for half a beat each (2 and &). So the first measure is counted 1–2 &–3–4.

In the upper second measure of the "Preparatory Drill," the first *quarter note* is tied to the next *eighth note.* It is counted 1 &–2, or 1½ beats. If you count by tapping your foot, the first quarter note is held for the downbeat and upbeat of beat 1, but, because of the tie, it is also held for the downbeat of beat 2. On the upbeat of beat 2, the second *eighth note* is played. Beats 3 and 4 are both *quarter notes* and are counted 3–4.

In the *lower* second measure of the "Preparatory Drill," the *dotted quarter note* is equal in time value to the *quarter note* tied to an *eighth note* in the *upper* second measure. The net effect for both measures is the same. The only difference between the upper and lower measures is the way they are written. They should sound exactly the same. In terms of counting and value of the notes, the third measure of the "Preparatory Drill" is the same as the second measure.

COCKLES AND MUSSELS (PAGES 64–65)

"Cockles and Mussels" is in ¾ time and begins with a pickup on beat 3. A dotted quarter note appears on beat 2 of the first full measure, and it is followed be an eighth note on the & after 3; play on 1, 2, and the last & in the measure.

The second full measure has a very interesting rhythm. There is an eighth note on beat 1 and a dotted quarter note on the &, which is held through beat 2 and the first part of 3. Finally, there is an eighth note on the & after beat 3. The measure is counted 1–&, (2–3) &. The rhythms in measures 1 and 2 are repeated exactly in measures 3 and 4, and then again in measures 5 and 6.

CLEMENTINE (PAGES 66–67)

"Clementine," an American Western folk ballad, uses eighth notes in every measure except the last. It is in ¾ time and uses a pickup measure. Count 1–2 and play eighth notes on 3–&. In fact, beat 3 of every complete measure is eighth notes. Additional lyrics are provided on page 67.

CHORDS USED IN THIS SONG

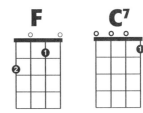

GO TELL AUNT RHODY

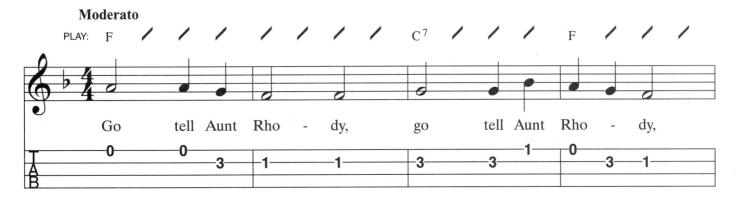

Go tell Aunt Rho - dy, go tell Aunt Rho - dy,

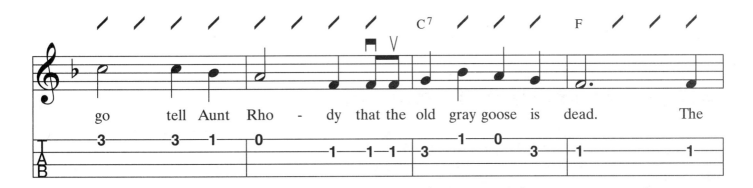

go tell Aunt Rho - dy that the old gray goose is dead. The

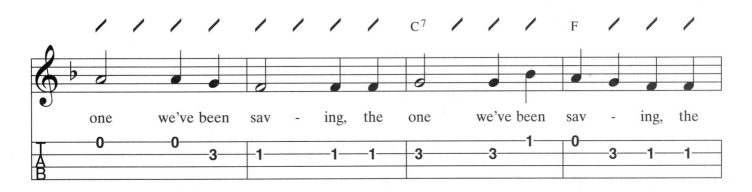

one we've been sav - ing, the one we've been sav - ing, the

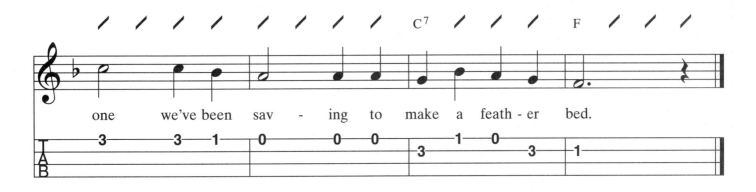

one we've been sav - ing to make a feath - er bed.

Dotted Quarter Notes

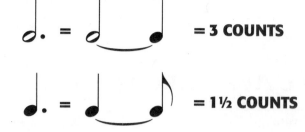

**A DOT INCREASES
THE LENGTH OF A NOTE
BY ONE HALF**

Preparatory Drill

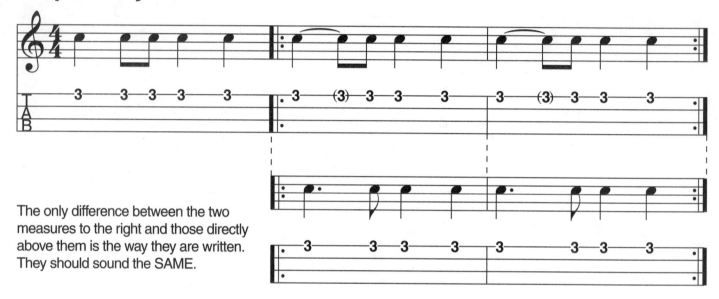

The only difference between the two measures to the right and those directly above them is the way they are written. They should sound the SAME.

CHORDS USED IN THIS SONG

COCKLES AND MUSSELS

Track 43
Vocals & Chords

Track 44
Chords Only

Moderately

In Dub-lin's fair cit-y, where girls are so pret-ty, I first set my eyes on sweet Mol-ly Ma-lone, As she

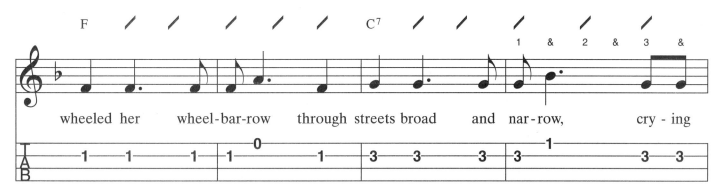

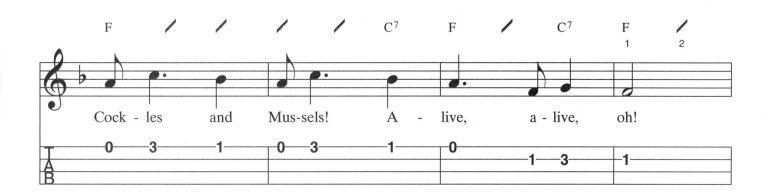

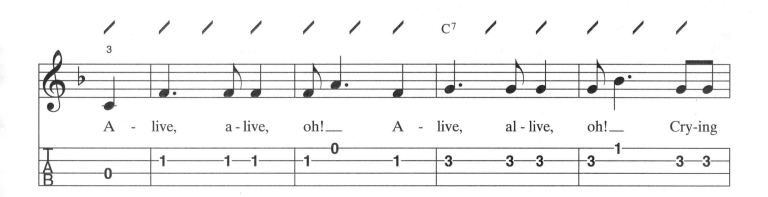

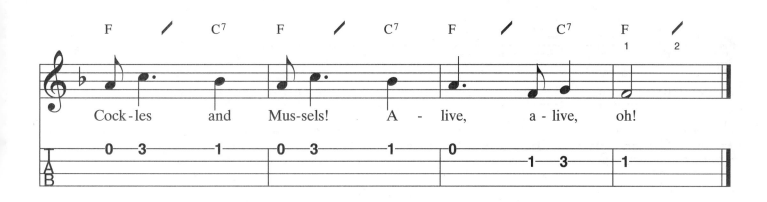

CHORDS USED IN THIS SONG

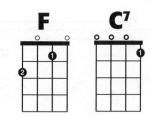

CLEMENTINE

Track 45 Vocals & Chords   Track 46 Chords Only

Moderately fast

In a cav - ern, in a can - yon, ex - ca - vat - ing for a

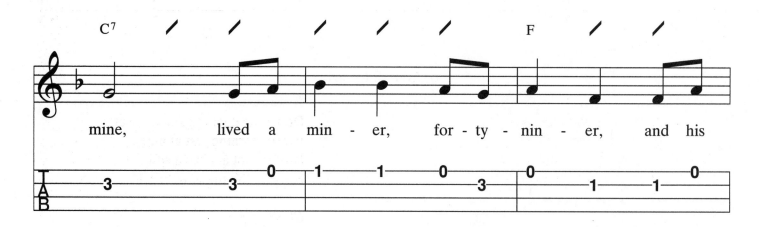

mine, lived a min - er, for - ty - nin - er, and his

daugh - ter, Clem - en - tine. Oh my dar - lin', oh my

dar - lin', oh my dar - lin', Clem-en - tine, you are

lost and gone for - ev - er; Dread-ful sor - ry, Clem-en - tine.

Additional Lyrics

Verse 2:
Light she was and like a fairy,
And her shoes were number nine,
Herring boxes, without topses,
Sandals were for Clementine.

Chorus:
Oh my darling, oh my darling,
Oh my darling Clementine!
Thou art lost and gone forever,
Dreadful sorry, Clementine.

Verse 3:
Drove she ducklings to the water,
Every morning just at nine,
Hit her foot against a splinter,
Fell into the foaming brine.

Chorus:
Oh my darling, oh my darling,
Oh my darling Clementine!
Thou art lost and gone forever,
Dreadful sorry, Clementine.

Verse 4:
Ruby lips above the water,
Blowing bubbles soft and fine,
But, alas, I was no swimmer,
So I lost my Clementine.

Chorus:
Oh my darling, oh my darling,
Oh my darling Clementine!
Thou art lost and gone forever,
Dreadful sorry, Clementine.

The G7 Chord

The G7 chord uses three left-hand fingers. Place your 2nd finger on the 2nd fret of the 3rd string, your 1st finger on the 1st fret of the 2nd string, and your 3rd finger on the 2nd fret of the 1st string. Look at the chord diagram and photograph at the top of page 69.

Turning your wrist slightly to the left, so the thumb side of your hand is closer to the neck, will help you get all three fingers directly next to their frets. Play on the tips of your fingers and be sure to touch only one string with each one; avoid accidentally bumping an adjacent string. Slowly pluck each string and make sure they are all ringing clearly.

The examples on page 69 combine the G7 chord with the other chords you know in $\frac{2}{4}$, $\frac{3}{4}$, and $\frac{4}{4}$ time. As always, strive to keep your movements smooth, direct, and small.

Aloha 'Oe (page 70)

"Aloha 'Oe" is Queen Lili'uokalani's (Hawaii's last monarch) most famous song and is an important part of Hawaii's cultural heritage. This arrangement uses just chords, so you can focus on getting used to the G7 chord. It will be fun to sing along, so listen to the recording to learn the tune if you don't know it, and play along if you like.

The *rhythmic notation* slashes ⎰ indicate to strum quarter notes.

When the Saints Go Marching In (page 71)

One of the most popular songs ever written, "The Saints," as it's often called, is a treat for both performers and the audience. It includes more examples of tied notes. In measure 12, the dotted half note, which is tied to a half note, is played on beat 2, so your count starts on that number and will be 2–3–4, 1–2 (*not* 2–3–4–5–6). In the first tie of the song near the top of the page, where the whole note is tied to a quarter note, your count would be 1–2–3–4, 1 (*not* 1–2–3–4–5). Also, notice that because there's a three-beat pickup, the last measure only contains one beat

"When the Saints Go Marching In" is an old gospel hymn and, in its original form, doesn't sound much like what we're used to hearing today. In the early 1920s, Dixieland jazz musicians doubled the note values, sped up the tempo, and a jazz standard was born. To this day, it remains the most-requested Dixieland jazz song.

Notice the tempo is allegro, so strive for a spritely pace. There are lots of long, tied notes and notes *decay* (get soft) quickly on a ukulele, so it's important to practice this until you can play it quickly.

The G7 Chord

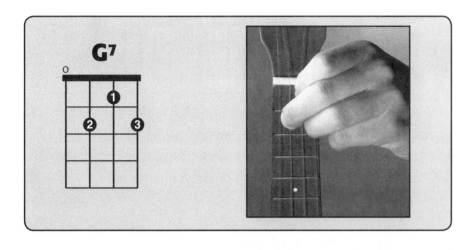

OTHER CHORDS ON THIS PAGE

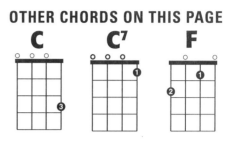

Place your 1st, 2nd, and 3rd fingers in position,
then play one string at a time.

Play all four strings
together:

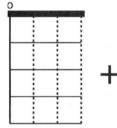 + 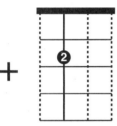 + 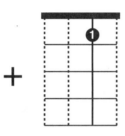 + 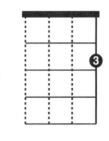 =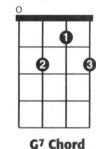

Track 48

Play slowly and evenly.

1. 𝄞 4/4 G7 / / / | C / / / | G7 / / / | C / / / |

2. 𝄞 3/4 C / / | G7 / / | C / / | G7 / / | C / / | C 𝄽 𝄽 ‖

3. 𝄞 2/4 G7 / | C / | G7 / | C / | F / | C / | G7 / | C / ‖

4. 𝄞 4/4 C / / / | F / / / | C / / / | G7 / / / | C / / / | C / / 𝄽 ‖

5. 𝄞 3/4 C / / | C7 / / | F / / | C / / | F / / | F / / | C / / | C / / |

G7 / / | G7 / / | C / / | F / / | C / / | C 𝄽 𝄽 ‖

CHORDS USED IN THIS SONG

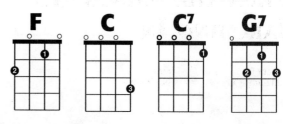

ALOHA 'OE
(Farewell to Thee)  Track 49

To get used to playing the G7 chord, play this version of "Aloha 'Oe" (pronounced "oy") with just chords. Sing along with the melody.

This arrangement uses quarter note slashes ♩ that indicate to play one strum on each quarter note.

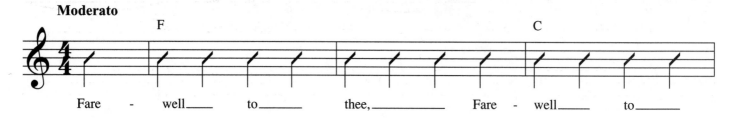

Fare - well____ to____ thee,____ Fare - well____ to____

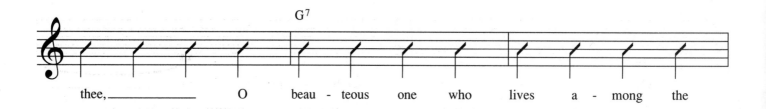

thee,_____ O beau - teous one who lives a - mong the

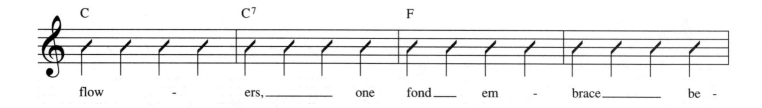

flow - ers,____ one fond____ em - brace____ be -

fore____ I____ leave,_____ un - til_____ we

meet____ a - gain.____

WHEN THE SAINTS GO MARCHING IN

Track 50 Melody & Chords Track 51 Chords Only

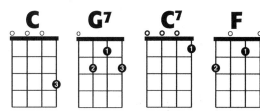

CHORDS USED IN THIS SONG

Allegro

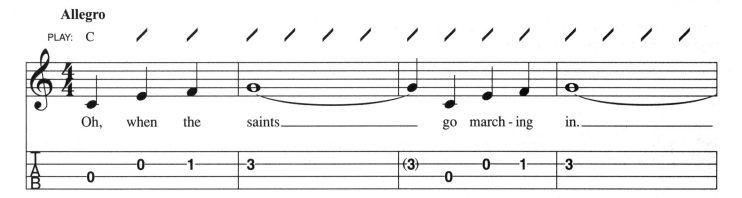

Oh, when the saints go march-ing in.

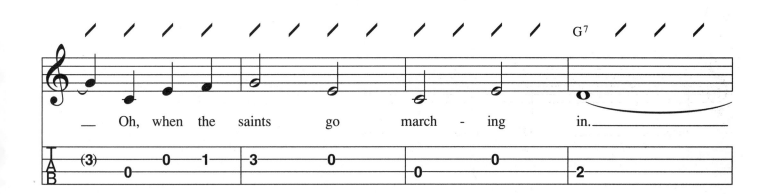

Oh, when the saints go march-ing in.

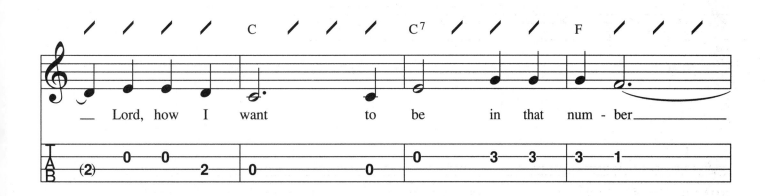

Lord, how I want to be in that num-ber

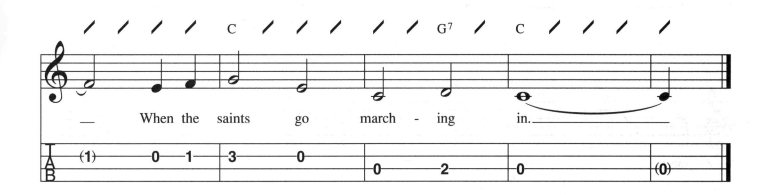

When the saints go march-ing in.

LOVE SOMEBODY

Like other songs in this book, this American folk song is arranged so that you can play it two different ways. First, you can play it as a solo ukulele piece, playing the notes as written. Notice the extensive use of the C and G7 chords. Because this is a folk song about love, modify your picking style to a softer, gentler sound. When playing the melody, remember to use alternate picking on the eighth notes, which happen in the seventh and fourteenth measures.

Another way to play the song is to accompany yourself by strumming the chords as you sing the melody. The chords are C and G7. When playing "Love Somebody," you'll alternate strumming C four times, then G7 four times, then C four times, and so on. For the first eight measures, this pattern is only broken in measure 7 where you strum C twice followed by G7 twice.

Singing while you strum the chords is one of the best things about playing the ukulele and is well worth the extra effort. Get to know the melody by playing the notes as written. Then pick **C** on the 2nd string. This **C** is your starting note when you start to sing. Try not to look at your hands.

As you start to sing, look at the music page for the lyrics and for the chord symbols. It is a simple song, so you should be able to memorize it quickly. There is a repeat sign at the end of the song, so play and sing it twice. Count evenly by tapping your foot. You may not be ready for prime-time TV, but you're a lot closer than when you started this book, 71 pages ago.

THE STREETS OF LAREDO (PAGE 74)

In this cowboy ballad, also known as "The Cowboy's Lament," a dying cowboy tells his life story to a younger one. It is in $\frac{3}{4}$ time and starts with a pickup on beat 3, which is why the very last measure has only two beats.

"The Streets of Laredo" uses most of the notes you know, and just the C and G7 chords. You can play the melody part, or strum the chords and sing the melody. Enjoy playing along with a friend, your teacher, or the recording.

Notice that the third line is exactly the same as the first, and the fourth line is very similar to the second. Noticing this will make it easier to learn. Also, pay special attention to the dotted-quarter note, eighth-note, quarter-note rhythm in the first full measure and in measure 9. It is counted 1 (&)–(2) &–3.

The Down-and-Up Stroke (PAGE 75)

So far, you have been strumming with quarter-note down-strokes. It works well, but adding eighth notes to your strumming will make your accompaniments more interesting.

When you pick individual eighth notes, you use alternate picking (pages 60–61). Strumming eighth notes is very similar to picking. To strum a pair of eighth notes, we use the *down-and-up stroke* strum, which can be thought of as *alternate strumming*. Usually, on an up-stroke strum, we play just the top two or three strings. It is possible to strum all four strings with an upstroke, but it will feel and sound more natural to strum up a little lighter, and only over the higher-sounding strings.

There are three examples on page 75. They all use a rhythm that has eighth notes on the first and second parts of the second beat: the 2 and the & after it. The rhythm has quarter notes on beats 1 and 3, so it is counted 1–2 &–3. In the first exercise, play and count the rhythm just once. Try counting and feeling a full $\frac{3}{4}$ measure of eighth notes before stumming a C chord and counting the rhythm. In the second exercise, count yourself in and play the rhythm on a C chord and follow it with a G7 chord in the same rhythm. Finally, in the third exercise, you'll play the rhythm for four full measures, switching from C to G7, and back to C.

When you're comfortable with the third exercise, try strumming through "The Streets of Laredo" on page 74 using this rhythm. Then, try it with any or all the $\frac{3}{4}$ songs you have learned! Have fun!

CHORDS USED IN THIS SONG

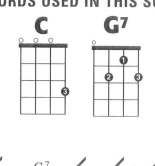

LOVE SOMEBODY

 Track 52
Vocals & Chords

 Track 53
Chords Only

Moderately

Love some-bod-y, yes, I do; Love some-bod-y, yes, I do;

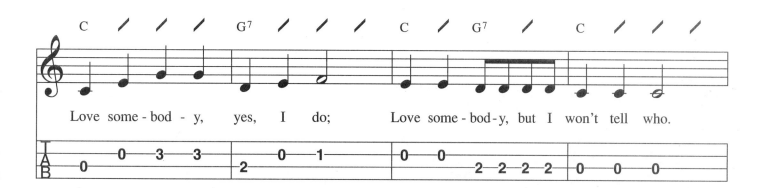

Love some-bod-y, yes, I do; Love some-bod-y, but I won't tell who.

Love some-bod-y, yes, I do; Love some-bod-y, yes, I do;

Love some-bod-y, yes, I do; And I hope some-bod-y loves me too.

THE STREETS OF LAREDO

CHORDS USED IN THIS SONG

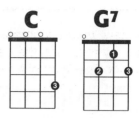

Track 54
Vocals & Chords

Track 55
Chords Only

Moderately

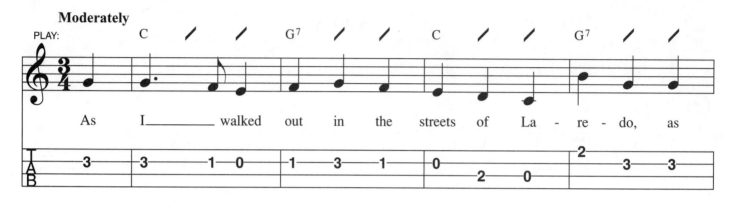

As I_____ walked out in the streets of La - re - do, as

I walked out in La - re - do one day, I

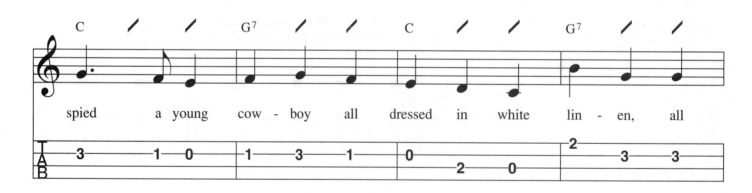

spied a young cow - boy all dressed in white lin - en, all

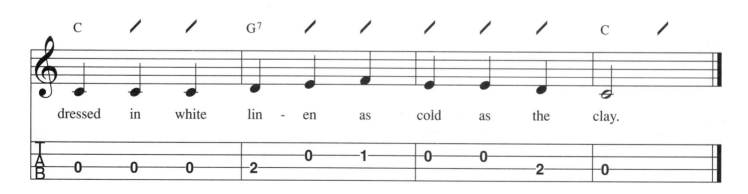

dressed in white lin - en as cold as the clay.

The Down-and-Up Stroke

You can make your accompaniment of waltz songs in $\frac{3}{4}$ like "The Streets of Laredo" more interesting by replacing the second beat of the measure with a down-stroke followed by an up-stroke. The symbol for down-stroke is ⊓; an up-stroke uses the symbol ⋁. Together, the down-and-up strokes are played in the same time as a regular strum.

Try the following exercise to first just work on the new rhythm.

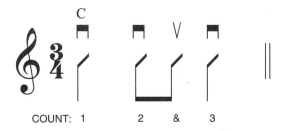

Now practice changing from C to G7.

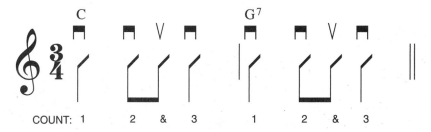

Now practice changing back and forth from C to G7 and back. When you can do it smoothly, go back to page 74 and use it to accompany "The Streets of Laredo."

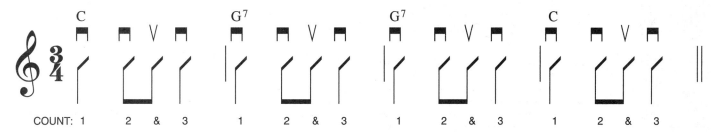

The Fermata

On the top of page 77, you will see an odd-looking sign. Some musicians refer to it as a "bird's eye." Its more formal name is *fermata,* an Italian word that means *hold.* When you see a fermata sign above (or sometimes below) a note, hold the note for approximately twice its usual number of beats or counts. Depending on the music, you have the option of slowing down a little before you play the held note—it's your choice. This is a good opportunity to exercise your growing musical judgment.

MICHAEL, ROW THE BOAT ASHORE

This spiritual from the time of the Civil War is in $\frac{4}{4}$ time and has a two-beat pickup measure. Count 1–2 and start playing on 3. The melody uses the dotted-quarter note/eighth-note rhythm, followed by two quarter notes. You'll find this in the first full measure and the fifth measure.

Although this last measure has only two beats to balance out the two-beat pickup measure, you'll hold the last note for another two beats because of the fermata on the last note.

After mastering "The Streets of Laredo" on page 74, "Michael, Row the Boat Ashore" will be easy! It uses the C, F, and G7 chords. Enjoy both playing the melody and strumming the chords. Play along with the recording or sing the song and accompany yourself.

Be sure to use a thorough practice routine.

1. Look over every new piece first to observe all of the important features, especially repeated musical ideas, new notes, and rhythms.

2. Learn to count and clap the rhythms.

3. Practice saying the names of the notes aloud in rhythm as you tap your foot on every beat.

4. Practice saying the finger numbers aloud in rhythm as you tap your foot on every beat.

5. Use additive practice. Practice playing slowly, just two measures at a time until they feel easy to play. Then, do the same with the next two measures. When they feel easy to play, play all four measures. Learn two more measures, then play all six. Continue this way through the whole piece.

The Fermata

This sign is called a *fermata*. It means to hold the note it is over a little longer.

CHORDS USED IN THIS SONG
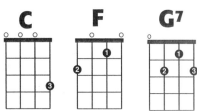

MICHAEL, ROW THE BOAT ASHORE

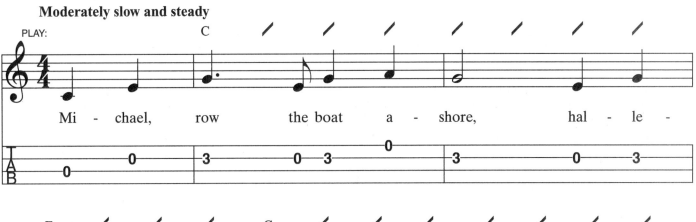

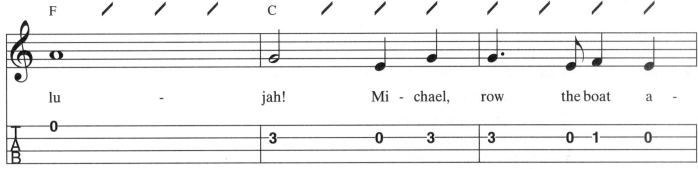

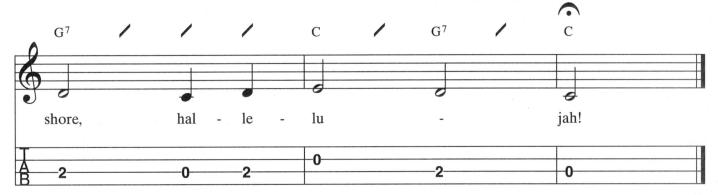

Additional Lyrics

Verse 2:
Sister, help to trim the sail, hallelujah!
Sister, help to trim the sail, hallelujah!

Chorus:
Michael, row the boat ashore, hallelujah!
Michael, row the boat ashore, hallelujah!

Verse 3:
Jordan's river is chilly and cold, hallelujah!
Jordan's river is chilly and cold, hallelujah!

Chorus:
Michael, row the boat ashore, hallelujah!
Michael, row the boat ashore, hallelujah!

FRANKIE AND JOHNNY

"Frankie and Johnny" is a popular American song from the late 1800s. The lyrics describe the story of how a woman named Frankie took revenge on her two-timing husband, Johnny. It uses all the notes and chords you have learned, as well as ties and the quarter rest.

Look at the first measure and notice the tie from the fourth eighth note to the fifth. You'll play an **A** on the & after 2, hold the note through 3, and then play a **G** on the & after 3. The measure is counted 1 &–2 &–(3) &–4. This exact rhythm also happens in the third and fifth measures. Something similar happens in the second measure. The second eighth note is tied to a dotted half note. The measure is counted 1 &–2, then you'll hold for the remainder of the measure.

Another interesting rhythm happens in the ninth and tenth measures. The whole-note **D** in the ninth measure (end of the third line) is tied to an eighth-note **D** on the first beat of the tenth measure (beginning of the fourth line). Then you'll resume playing with eighth notes starting with the **A** on the & after 1.

When a new song or piece includes complicated rhythms, it's a good idea to practice counting aloud and clapping the rhythm you're going to be playing. That way, you'll be confident about the rhythm when it's time to also pay attention to playing the notes. For instance, to practice the rhythms in measures 1, 3, and 5, clap this rhythm:

Repeat this rhythm until it is completely comfortable for you to clap. Then play those measures on just one open string, and finally with the written notes. Start slowly and speed up.

Practice carefully.

1. Look over every new piece first to observe all of the important features, especially repeated musical ideas, new notes, and rhythms.

2. Learn to count and clap the rhythms.

3. Practice saying the names of the notes aloud in rhythm as you tap your foot on every beat.

4. Practice saying the finger numbers aloud in rhythm as you tap your foot on every beat.

5. Use additive practice to learn to play this song. It's the quickest way to learn! Practice playing slowly, just two measures at a time until they feel easy to play. Then, do the same with the next two measures. When they feel easy to play, play all four measures. Learn two more measures, then play all six. Continue this way through the whole piece.

Frankie and Johnny

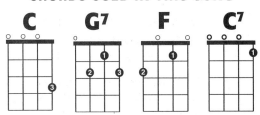

CHORDS USED IN THIS SONG

Moderate blues tempo

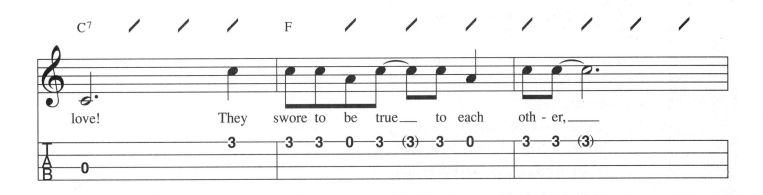

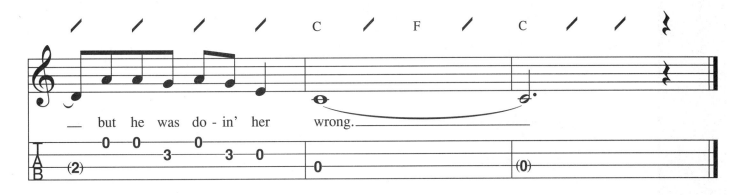

16th Notes

On pages 18 and 19, you learned about whole notes, half notes, and quarter notes. A whole note gets four beats, a half note gets two, and a quarter note gets one. So, a half note is half the value of a whole note, and a quarter note is half the value of a half note. On pages 60–61, you learned the eighth note, which gets half a beat and is thus half the value of a quarter note.

These are *16th notes:*

A 16th note is half the value of an eighth note, so two 16th notes equal one eighth note, and four 16th notes equal a quarter note. They are counted 1 e & a–2 e & a, etc. This chart makes the relationships of the note values clear:

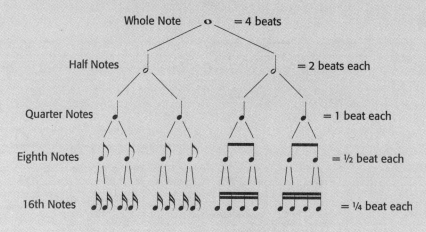

The Dotted Eighth and 16th Note Rhythm

As you know, a dot following a note increases the value of the note by one half. So, a dotted half note is three beats (like a half note tied to a quarter note, 2+1), and a dotted quarter note is one-and-a-half beats (like a quarter note tied to an eighth note, 1+½). So, a dotted eighth note equals ¾ of a beat (like an eighth note tied to a 16th note, ½+¼).

A dotted eighth note is usually followed by a single 16th note (connected to the eighth note with a beam) to create the dotted eighth and 16th note rhythm.

Carefully study the top half of page 81. Slowly count aloud and clap the first two rhythm examples provided, then repeat "hump-ty dump-ty" as you clap the rhythm.

Blues Strum

Using the down-and-up stroke you learned on page 75, play the "Blues Strum" as you count aloud, or repeat "hump-ty dump-ty." Remember that up-strokes can be lighter than down-strokes and only require that you include the the first two or three strings. A good variation on this rhythm is shown here. Have fun with this new sound!

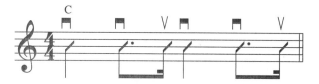

The Dotted Eighth and 16th Note Rhythm

Like eighth notes, dotted eighths and 16ths are played two to each beat. But unlike eighth notes (which are played evenly) dotted eighths and 16ths are played *unevenly*: long, short, long, short.

Compare the following:

An easy way to remember the sound of dotted eighths and 16ths is to say the words:

"hump - ty dump - ty hump - ty dump - ty"

The dotted eighth and 16th note rhythm is very common in all kinds of music, but **especially classical, folk, country, and blues.**

Blues Strum Track 61

You can make your accompaniment of songs like "Frankie and Johnny" more interesting by using a blues strum. Use the dotted eighth and 16th note rhythm. Each measure of ⁴⁄₄ time contains four down-strokes and four up-strokes.

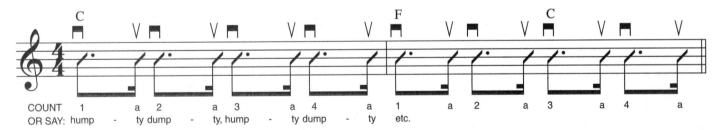

You can create a variation on the blues strum above by changing the notes on beats 1 and 3 to quarter notes, so the rhythm is quarter followed by dotted eighth and 16th. Repeat this pattern twice in each measure.

CARELESS LOVE

"Careless Love" is a traditional song that became a standard for both jazz and blues musicians. This song is offered here to give you more practice with the blues strum you learned on pages 80–81. No tablature is shown for the melody, because there are notes that can't be played on the ukulele. Strumming this song will require all four chords you know.

Strum along along with the recording, or sing the melody and accompany yourself. Have fun!

The G Chord (PAGE 84)

Like the G7 chord, the G chord uses three left-hand fingers. In fact, they are the same three fingers: the 1st, 2nd, and 3rd fingers, but they are used differently. Place your 1st finger on the 2nd fret of the 3rd string, your 2nd finger on the 2nd fret of the 1st string, and your 3rd finger on the 3rd fret of the 2nd string. Look at the chord diagram and photograph at the top of page 84.

As with the G7 chord, turning your wrist slightly to the left, so the thumb-side of your hand is closer to the neck, will help you get all three fingers directly next to their frets. Always play on the tips of your fingers and be sure to avoid accidentally bumping an adjacent string. Pluck each string and make sure they are all ringing clearly.

The first two examples on page 84 will give you some practice with the G chord in $\frac{2}{4}$ and $\frac{3}{4}$ time. The bottom three exercises combine the G chord with the other chords you know in $\frac{2}{4}$, $\frac{3}{4}$, and $\frac{4}{4}$ time. As always, strive to keep your movements, smooth, direct, and small.

The D7 Chord (PAGE 85)

The D7 chord has an important similarity to the G chord: it uses both the 1st and 2nd fingers on the 2nd fret. The important difference is that for the D7 chord, the fingers are placed on the 4th and 2nd strings instead of the 3rd and 1st. Also, only those two fingers are required, while the G chord uses three fingers. Look at the chord diagram and photograph at the top of page 85.

Since D7 does have two fingers on the same fret, it is helpful to turn your wrist to the left and allow both fingers to be positioned directly next to their frets. Also, since there are open strings adjacent to both fretted strings, be sure to use the very tips of the fingers and avoid bumping into an adacent string, which would prevent it from vibrating. All four strings need to vibrate freely so every note in the chord can be heard clearly.

The first two exercises in the middle of page 85 will give you some practice with the D7 chord in $\frac{2}{4}$ and $\frac{3}{4}$ time. The three exercises at the bottom of the page combine D7 with the chords you know. When switching between D7 and G, keep in mind the similarity of their fingerings: the 1st and 2nd fingers will maintain the same "shape" in both chords—just add the 3rd finger for the G chord, and remove it for the D7. This is a great example of why it is very important to keep your fingers close to the strings when you aren't using them; when switching between these two chords, your 3rd finger should remain close by so it's easy to press it down again when it's time to play the G chord.

CHORDS USED IN THIS SONG

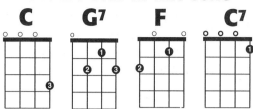

C   G7   F   C7

CARELESS LOVE Track 62

The blues strum will work nicely for this song. Notice the melody of "Careless Love" has notes you don't know. Many lead sheets you play from will contain notes that you can't play on the ukulele. If that is the case, just play the chords and sing along!

Moderate blues tempo

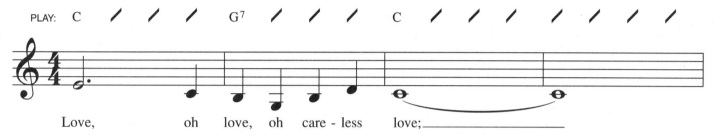

Love,   oh love, oh care - less   love;_____

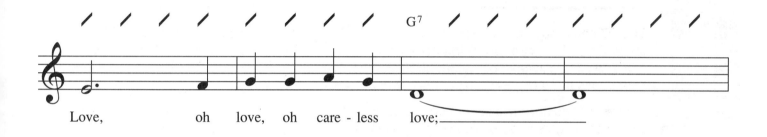

Love,   oh love, oh care - less   love;_____

Love,   oh love,   oh care - less   love;   just

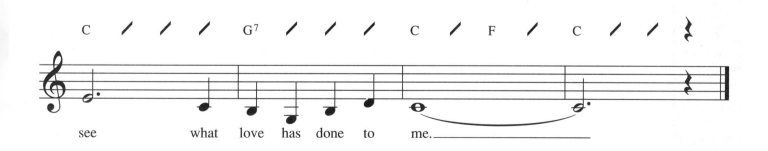

see   what love has done to   me._____

The G Chord 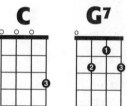 Track 63

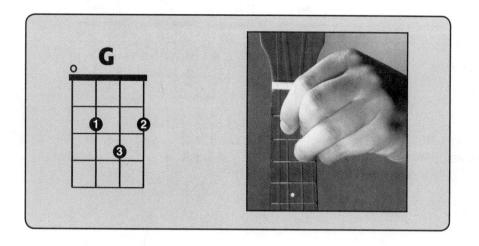

OTHER CHORDS ON THIS PAGE

C   **G⁷**

Place your 1st, 2nd, and 3rd fingers in position, then play one string at a time.

Play all four strings together:

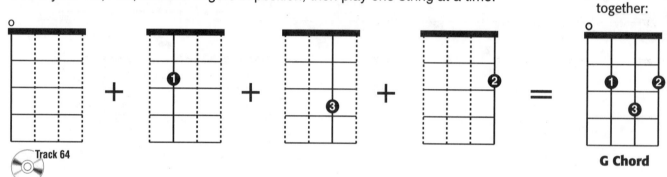

Track 64

G Chord

Play slowly and evenly.

Track 65

Repeat each line several times.

The D7 Chord

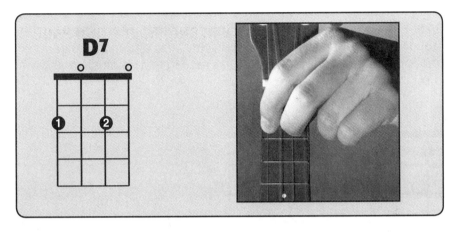

OTHER CHORDS ON THIS PAGE

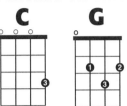

Place your 1st and 2nd fingers in position, then play one string at a time.

Play all four strings together:

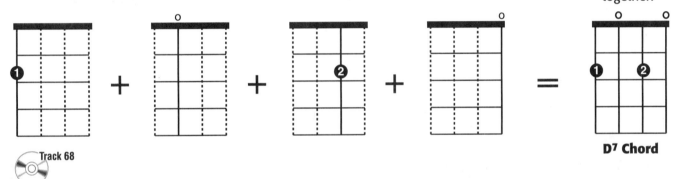

D7 Chord

Play slowly and evenly.

1. Play slowly and evenly with D7.

2. Play slowly and evenly with D7.

Repeat each line several times.

1. G ... D7 ... C ... D7 ... G

2. G ... C ... D7 ... C ... G

3. G ... G7 ... C ... D7 G ... C D7 ... G

Introducing F-Sharp (PAGE 88)

A *sharp* ♯ raises a note a half step, which equals one fret on a ukulele. F♯ (F-sharp) is played one fret higher than the note F. Since F is played on the 1st fret of the 2nd string, F♯ is played on the 2nd fret. When a sharp note appears in a measure, it is still sharp until the end of that measure. Notice that, although we put the sharp sign after the name of the note in text, in music notation, the sign appears directly before the note head.

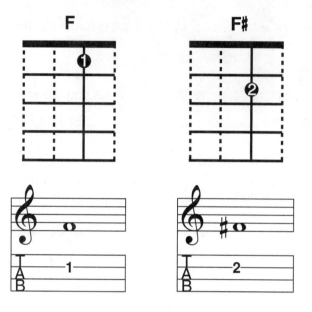

LITTLE BROWN JUG (PAGES 88–89)

This 19th century drinking song became popular during the Prohibition era. The arrangement offered here is a chance for you to practice strumming the D7 chord you learned on page 85. Playing the melody would be a fun way to practice playing the F♯, but to play it, you would need to change the low B notes in measures 1 and 5 to D's, because that low B is not playable on a ukulele. You will get to play the F♯ in "Over the Rainbow" on pages 100–101.

For now, focus on mastering the D7 chord. Make an exercise of switching from D7 to G, and back again before strumming through the song. Think about maintaining the relative positions of the 1st and 2nd finger as you shift them over from the 4th and 2nd strings (for D7) to the 3rd and 1st strings (for G). As always, don't press down any harder than necessary, and keep your movements small and direct.

Bluegrass Strum (PAGE 89)

Using the down-and-up stroke you learned on page 75 in a bluegrass strum will spice up your accompaniments. Practice the bluegrass strum exercise at the bottom of page 89, and then try it in your rendition of "Little Brown Jug."

D.C. al Fine (PAGE 90)

D.C. stands for *da capo* (dah-CAH-po), which means "from the beginning." *Fine* (FEE-nay) means "the end." When you see *D.C. al Fine*, go back to the beginning and play to the *Fine* marking. This is one of several tools musicians use to indicate that a section of music is to be repeated. *D.C. al Fine* is used in cases where some of the music is repeated, but not all.

When you get to the *D.C. al Fine* marking in the music, go back to the very beginning without pausing—keep your rhythm steady—and then play until you see the "Fine" indication, which is the end.

Gimme That Old-Time Religion (pages 90–91)

"Gimme That Old-Time Religion" is a traditional Southern gospel song dating back to the late 1800s. It starts with a pickup (pages 56–57) on beat 3. Count 1–2, and start playing on 3. The dotted quarter, eighth-note rhythm (page 64) appears several times. This is a fun song that is fairly easy to play. Just make sure you have mastered the rhythms before playing. Practice counting aloud and clapping first.

Always use a thorough practice regimen:

1. Look over every new piece first to observe all of the important features, especially repeated musical ideas, new notes, and rhythms.

2. Learn to count and clap the rhythms.

3. Practice saying the names of the notes aloud in rhythm as you tap your foot on every beat.

4. Practice saying the finger numbers aloud in rhythm as you tap your foot on every beat.

5. Use additive practice to learn to play this song. It's the quickest way to learn! Practice playing slowly, just two measures at a time until they feel easy to play. Then, do the same with the next two measures. When they feel easy to play, play all four measures. Learn two more measures, then play all six. Continue this way through the whole piece.

Here are some additional lyrics for "Gimme That Old-Time Religion":

It was good for our mothers,…

Makes me love everybody,…

It was good for our fathers,…

It was good for Paul and Silas,…

It will do when I am dying,…

It was good for the prophet Daniel,…

It was tried in the fiery furnace,…

It will take us all to heaven,…

Introducing F-Sharp 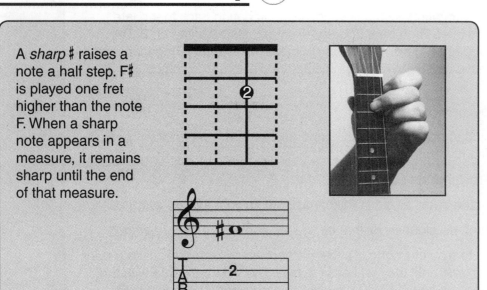 Track 69

A *sharp* ♯ raises a note a half step. F♯ is played one fret higher than the note F. When a sharp note appears in a measure, it remains sharp until the end of that measure.

F♯

LITTLE BROWN JUG

Track 70
Vocals & Chords

Track 71
Chords Only

Track 72
Chords Only in
Bluegrass Strum

CHORDS USED IN THIS SONG

G   C   D7

Brightly

PLAY: G / / /   C / / /   D7 / / /

My wife and I live all a - lone in a lit-tle brown hut we

G / / / / / / /   C / / /

call our own;   she loves gin, and I love rum, I

tell you what, don't we have fun? Ha, ha, ha, you and me,

lit - tle brown jug, don't I love thee? Ha, ha, ha,

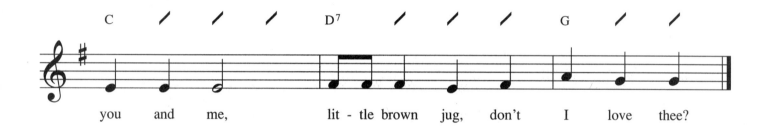

you and me, lit - tle brown jug, don't I love thee?

Bluegrass Strum Track 73

You can make your accompaniment to "Little Brown Jug" and other country favorites more interesting by using a bluegrass strum. This strum breaks up the steady four-beats-to-the-measure with up-strokes on the second and fourth beats. Try the exercise below, and when you can do it smoothly, apply it to "Little Brown Jug."

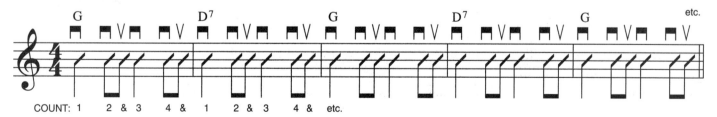

COUNT: 1   2 & 3   4 &   1   2 & 3   4 &   etc.

D.C. al Fine

D.C. al Fine stands for the Italian expression "Da Capo al Fine" (dah CAH-po al FEE-nay).
It means to go back to the beginning of the song and play as far as the word "Fine,"
which is the end of the song.

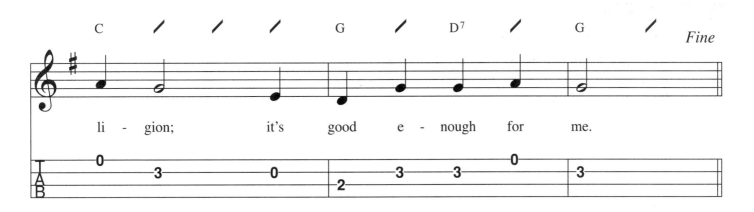

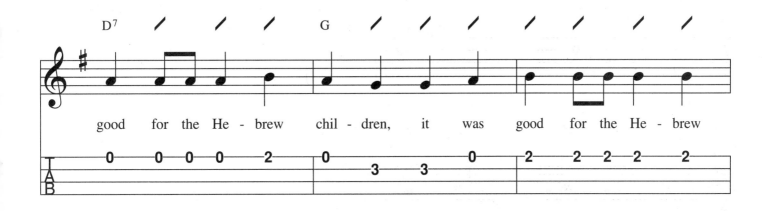

Calypso Strum

Calypso is Afro-Caribbean music that originated in Trinidad and Tobago during the first half of the 20th century. It draws upon African and French influences and is characterized by very rhythmic vocals, most often sung in a French.

Calypso rhythms are a little *syncopated*, which makes them a bit tricky to play, at first. *Syncopation* is music played off the strong part of the beat—the stress is moved to the weak part. In other words, instead of starting a rhythm on the first part of the count, such as on 3, we might be silent on 3 (notice the *eighth rest* ❼ on beat 3 of every measure) and play on &, instead. The three examples on page 93 will prepare you to play calypso rhythms, so take your time studying and mastering them, especially the third one, before continuing.

MARY ANN (PAGE 94)

The Caribbean folk song "Mary Ann" provides a great opportunity for you to practice your calypso strumming. You can also learn to play the melody. Have a friend or your teacher strum the chords in a calypso rhythm while you play the tune, or play along with the recording. The whole rests will let the calypso strumming rhythm shine.

The tune is very easy to play. Just be sure to notice the tie in the measures 3, 7, 11, and 15. You'll be playing a note on the & after 2, and holding it through beats 3 and 4.

Be sure to take your turn as the calypso strummer! Have your friend or teacher play the melody (or play along with the recording) while you create the feel of the Caribbean islands.

THE SLOOP JOHN B. (PAGES 96–97)

This old folk song from Nassau, Bahamas was first published in 1916, and The Beach Boys made it a hit in 1966! This is another opportunity to use your calypso-style strumming. You'll start by strumming for four measures, then begin singing the melody on beat 4 of the fourth measure. Additional verses are provided on the bottom of page 97. Have fun!

Calypso Strum

Track 76

The calypso strum is used to accompany Caribbean songs like "Mary Ann,"
"Jamaica Farewell," and "The Sloop John B." The rhythm is a little tricky, so make
sure you can play the exercises on this page before trying the songs.

Play steady quarter notes on a C chord. Use only down-strokes.

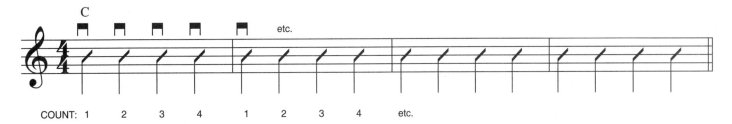

Now add an up-stroke after each down-stroke. Notice how
the count has changed.

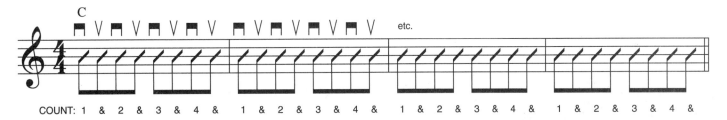

Now leave out the down-stroke on 3 and replace it with silence. Notice that you now
have two up-strokes in a row on the & of 2 and the & of 3.

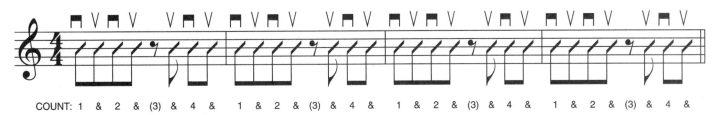

This whole third example is a repeated one-measure calypso-strum pattern. As soon
as you can do it without missing a beat, try "Mary Ann."

MARY ANN

 Track 77 Vocals & Chords   Track 78 Chords Only

The calypso strum is perfect for this song.

CHORDS USED IN THIS SONG

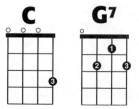

Moderately

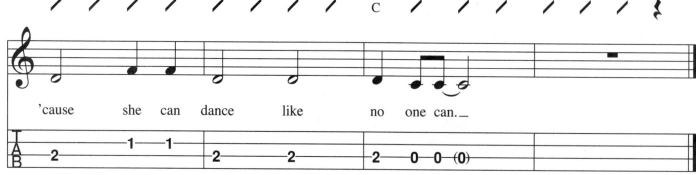

Here are some additional lyrics for "Mary Ann":

Additional Verses

Verse 2
Oh, when she walks long the shore people all she greets,
Wild birds fly her over and fish come to her feet.
In her heart there's love but I'm the only man,
Who's allowed to kiss my, oh Mary Ann.

Verse 3
All day all night is Mary Ann,
Down by the seaside, sifting sand.
Even little children love Mary Ann,
Down by the seaside, sifting sand.

Verse 4
Oh, when we marry we will have the time we ever thought,
I would be so happy, I'd kiss my mother-in-law.
All the little children running in the bamboo hut,
One for every palmtree and the coconut.

Verse 5
All day all night is Mary Ann,
Down by the seaside, sifting sand.
Even little children love Mary Ann,
Down by the seaside, sifting sand.

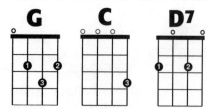

THE SLOOP JOHN B.

Start this song with the calypso strum to get into the rhythm of it.
Then start singing.

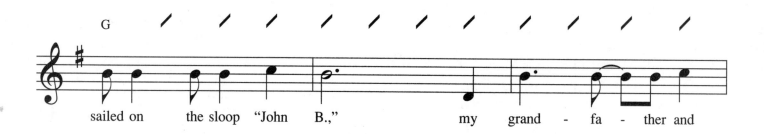

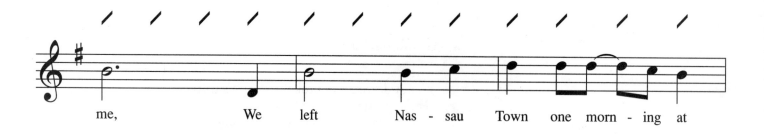

dawn.＿＿＿＿＿＿ I want＿ to go home,＿＿＿＿

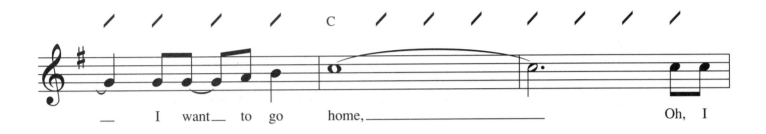

＿ I want＿ to go home,＿＿＿＿ Oh, I

feel so break＿ up I want＿ to go home.＿＿＿

Additional Verses

Verse 2:
The first mate he got drunk, and broke the capn's trunk,
The constable had to come and take him away.
Sheriff John Stone, why don't you leave me alone?
Yeah, yeah. Well I feel so broke up, I wanna go home.

Verse 3:
The poor cook he caught the fits, and threw away all my grits,
And then he took and he ate up all of my corn.
Let me go home, why don't they let me go home?
Yeah, yeah. This is the worst trip I've ever been on.

OVER THE RAINBOW (PAGES 100–101)

This beautiful song, written for the movie *The Wizard of Oz* and sung by a young Judy Garland, is a classic. It has been recorded and performed by so many artists that it is regarded an American "standard." It was recorded by the beloved Hawaiian ukulelist, Israel Kamakawiwo'Ole, known as "Iz," in 1993, in a *medley* (a combination of two or more different songs) with "It's a Wonderful World." It was later released as a single and became a big hit.

Here's your chance to play the **F#** you learned on page 88. You'll find it on the second line of page 101, in the second measure. Notice that the sharp sign only appears before the first **F**-note in that measure, but all of the **F**-notes in that measure are played as **F#**.

Other important features of this melody are the $\frac{4}{4}$ time signature, dotted half notes, plenty of eighth notes, and ties. Remember that it is a good idea to look through a new song carefully before you play it to identify features such as these.

You can learn both the melody and the chords to this popular song. The chords used are C, C7, G, G7, D7, and F. The C7 appears on beat 4 of measure 2, and the F right after it on beat 1 of measure 3. So, make switching from C7 to F an exercise and master that chord change before strumming through the song. Practice it slowly at first, and work on moving smoothly with confidence. This song will sound great with the calypso strum.

If you find the song tricky to play, learn it two measures at a time, using additive practice. Count aloud and clap the rhythms. A slow, careful approach is the quickest way to learn something new. Never spend time playing with confusion or error. Reinforce confident, accurate playing, even if very slow. You'll be able to play it more quickly, sooner, that way.

Enjoy playing this monster ukulele hit!

Is This the End? What Comes Next?

You have just about finished the *Self-Teaching Basic Ukulele Course!* It wasn't so long ago that you were just getting started. Congratulations to you for sticking with the lessons and getting this far. We told you at the beginning that music has the potential to bring joy, pleasure, and relaxation into your life, and we hope that has proven to be the case.

This is not the end! But it is the end of the beginning. With the information you now have and the ability to play as well as you do, there is much music you are capable of performing. To progress further, there are several avenues you can follow. Look for the continuation of this book, *Alfred's Basic Ukulele Method,* Book 2, which continues in the same smoothly paced style but without the Study Guides.

There are also many other Alfred Music ukulele books that can improve your skills and introduce you to a world of different musical styles. Check out *Beginning Ukulele* (#40916) by Shana Aisenberg and Greg Horne, which includes an instructional DVD featuring the renowned, Grammy-winning ukulele player, Daniel Ho. This is followed up by *Intermediate Ukulele* (#40919) and *Mastering Ukulele* (#40922), both of which also include DVDs featuring Daniel Ho.

You can browse through great books and videos at our website: www.alfred.com/ukulele.

Other Ways to Learn

Though learning from a book by experienced ukulele players is an excellent way to proceed, you can go in a different direction. Many young ukulele players just go out into the world and meet other ukulele players to learn how to play more chords, more keys, more accompaniment styles, and how to move up and down the fingerboard. Just mingling with other ukulele players can be a wonderful learning experience—and sometimes, if you are lucky, they may just ask you to sit in and jam with their group.

You can also pick up a lot of information by going to music clubs where local bands are performing. Just listening to a performer you admire on a recording will help you become a better musician. Even going to one of the big-time concerts in your area to hear and see one of the true greats can be an interesting learning experience. In short, you can learn from almost anyone who performs professionally, whether they are well-known or not. By exposing yourself to a wide range of musicians, you will soon develop a style of playing and performing that will be uniquely yours.

Also, be sure to learn the chords shown on pages 112–118 of this book.

Becoming a Professional

For those of you who want to make a career of playing the ukulele and want to become a professional musician, you should consider taking lessons from a ukulele instructor. Personal one-on-one instruction will speed up your progress enormously. You'll be receiving immediate feedback on your playing and learning new techniques not easily available in any other way.

There is also the following bonus section, *Pathways to Becoming a Professional,* which advises you on a future career path. It starts on page 102 and ends on page 110, with nine pages of practical advice that, alone, is worth the price of this book. Anyone who aspires to a life in music should read this section very carefully. It contains down-to-earth instructions from someone who has been there and explains what you have to know and what you have to do. Keep this book close by because you'll be referring to this section again and again.

And now, it's time to say goodbye. It was great fun for us to prepare and write the Study Guides for you. In preparing them, we tried to picture a person who would buy this book—and luckily for us, it turned out to be you. May your life be forever enhanced by the music you make on your ukulele.

Self-Teaching Study Guide

CHORDS USED IN THIS SONG

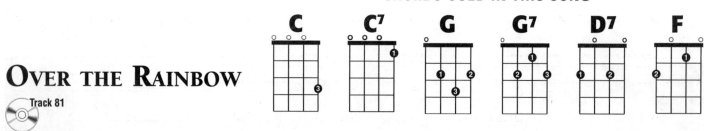

Over the Rainbow

Track 81

The greatest ukulele version of this song was recorded in 1993 by legendary Hawaiian uke player and singer Iz. This song will sound great with the calypso strum.

Words by E. Y. Harburg
Music by Harold Arlen

Bonus Section
PATHWAYS TO BECOMING A PROFESSIONAL

Though you do not have the skills to become a professional ukulele player now, it's not too early to think about what you have to do to become one. The music business has multiple parts to it and once having mastered your instrument, there will be many opportunities for you.

Teaching

Besides being a professional ukulelist playing in a band that is developing a following, there are a number of other things you can do. You could, for example, become a teacher. If you prefer to have a steady source of income while still being able to arrange your own hours, this could be for you. In addition to having a thorough knowledge of music theory and a high level of performance skills, it would be helpful to have a warm, engaging personality. If you're a person who likes people, this might be an excellent opportunity.

Selling and Repairing Ukuleles

There are many music stores that sell ukuleles who would probably welcome someone who is enthusiastic about their instrument and who would enjoy a job of selling ukuleles. Ukuleles need to be repaired from time to time, so if you are handy with tools, you might enjoy making repairs on instruments. There are also many very talented ukulelists who make themselves available for recording sessions, and if you live in an area where there are many studios and you become very good, this might appeal to you.

Performing on Weekends

You might also be someone who has a regular job but would still like to make some extra money by playing on weekends at birthday parties, weddings, cocktail hours, and other holiday events. Imagine a wedding on a beautiful Sunday afternoon in a park with a small group of musicians, including a ukulele player. They will play beautifully together and help make a wedding an unforgettable experience.

Playing Professionally

Because this book teaches you how to play, we will concentrate on the playing aspect of having a career. Playing the ukulele in a band is fun and rewarding. Even though you are not quite ready at this moment, it's important for you to understand what will be required of you when you are. As you gradually acquire the skills and knowledge to become a professional, there could be a day, and it could come at any moment, when you are in a club watching a band warm up and the main ukulelist turns to you and says, "Hey, kid, I need a break. Want to sit in for a couple of songs?" So being prepared for that moment is a requirement for getting started in a professional career.

The following section of *Pathways to Becoming a Professional* goes through the sequential steps you probably need to take to become a professional. We start with three pages of practice suggestions that are essential in getting you started, and then through the next steps, one by one, that will ultimately lead you to a professional career. You can read through this section all at once or read one section at a time as needed. So, let's first get started by organizing your practice sessions.

Practice

You may have heard this story that offers good advice for young musicians: Two young music students were visiting New York City. As this was their first time in the Big Apple, they did not know how to get around. So after getting a little lost, they asked a New York policeman, "How do you get to Carnegie Hall?" He looked at them sternly and said, "Practice, practice, practice."

Well, that probably never happened, but practice is essential to becoming a professional. The next three pages contain all you'll ever need to know to get the most out of your practice sessions and to become a professional.

Getting Warmed Up

One of the most important parts of a practice session is the warm-up. Playing vigorously without warming up can cause injury. Just as an athlete warms up before a strenuous workout, we must warm up our fingers before strenuous playing.

To warm up properly, all of the muscle groups you use to play should be warmed up slowly. Different muscle groups are used to play different things. Each of these different groups of muscles must be warmed up.

The key words for warming up are *slow* and *easy*. Let your hands gradually stretch out and get your circulation going. Start slowly and gradually increase the intensity of your playing. Starting slowly has two benefits. The first is that it allows your muscles to warm up gradually. The second is that it will keep you relaxed. Tight muscles are enemies of speed and accuracy.

Your warm-up routine could start with scales or picking exercises, then move to string bending and licks, and then finish with strumming. Warming up usually takes between 10 and 15 minutes but can vary depending on how often you play. The longer the periods of time between practice sessions, the longer (and slower) your warm-ups should be.

What to Practice

When you are deciding what to practice, consider both long-term and short-term goals as a player. Your short-term goal might be to learn a song that you like or to master a new technique. Your long-term goals may range from playing for a few friends to becoming a successful recording artist. Whatever your goals are, and they may change often, try to select areas of study that will help you reach your goals. If one of your goals is to become a well-rounded player, it is important to vary your areas of study and not work on the same things during each practice session. Here is a short list of things to consider:

Arpeggios	Memorizing Favorite Songs	Rhythm Ukulele
Bending and Vibrato	New Chords	Scales
Chords	Note Naming	Singing
Ear Training	Phrasing	Songwriting
Improvising	Playing While Standing	Technique Exercises
Lead Ukulele	Playing Songs from a Songbook	Timing and Rhythm
Learning New Songs	Practicing Songs that You Know	

Before you start practicing, try choosing three or four different areas that you would like to work on that day. Once you have selected them, make a list. Put them in order, starting with the area that you feel you need to focus on the most. You could even date the list, so that you can keep track of the areas you have been working on.

Keeping areas of study listed in order of priority will keep you from always playing the same things when you pick up your ukulele. It will also keep you focused on your goals. As you start to get bored with your work in one area, you can refer to your list and know exactly which area to focus on next.

If you don't get a chance to work on all of your selected areas one day, you may want to pick up where you left off during your next practice session. Make the last area you were working on the first during the next practice session.

Practice

How Much You Need to Practice to Become a Pro

In the early stages of learning to play, your practice time will most likely be shorter than when you become more advanced. As you gradually become more proficient, your practice time will necessarily increase. Most professional ukulelists practice several hours a day. If you would like to make a living playing the ukulele, plan to practice around 20 hours a week, or more. Around three hours a day is a good goal. Some days you'll have more time to play than others. But, if you want to play professionally, you'll want to make playing and practicing a high priority.

How Often Should You Practice

The more often you practice, the faster you'll improve. Try to pick up your ukulele at least once a day, five or six days a week, even if you only play for a few minutes. You'll find the more you play, the more you'll want to play.

How Much Practice Is Too Much

You are practicing too much when other parts of your life start to be neglected. No matter how badly you want to become a great ukulelist, you also need to have a life outside of the ukulele. Playing the ukulele can become an addiction. It can start to control your life instead of being a fun thing to do. Taking a day off every once in a while can actually be good for your playing.

In extreme cases, too much practice can even bring on repetitive stress injuries. If you are practicing several hours a day on a regular basis, then you need to be aware of repetitive stress injuries such as tendonitis. These injuries are often due to excess tension and strenuous playing without a proper warm-up.

Make Practice a Habit

In order to improve quickly, make practice a habit. If possible, practice at the same time each day. This is important for two reasons. The first is that things are easier to start if they are a habit. This is because you don't have to plan to do them—you just do them. For example, you don't have to plan to brush your teeth at night—you just do it. If you can make picking up your ukulele each day as automatic as brushing your teeth, you are bound to improve more quickly. The second reason is that if you play at the same time each day, you'll get into a groove where your schedule begins to form around this time. People will begin to know to leave you alone at that time of day.

How to Tell if You're Improving

A good way to gauge your progress is to record yourself playing, write the date on the recording, and then put it away for a few months. By making recordings every couple of months, you can compare recordings and objectively gauge your progress. Improvement comes slowly, and it can be hard to tell when or how much you are improving. Ironically, the more you play, the harder it is to tell if you are improving because when you're very good, improvement becomes very gradual. Just as it can be hard to notice when someone you see every day grows an inch over the course of a year, it can be difficult to notice improvement in your performance in less than a few months.

The Importance of Review

Reviewing what you have learned is an important part of learning to play. Each new thing that you learn builds on what you have learned in the past. Reviewing makes you more able to use the things you've learned by keeping them fresh in your mind. It speeds up the learning process. It will save you from spending time re-learning things. Every month, devote a day or two of practice to review what you've learned in the past few months.

Practice

Practice Standing Up

If you are a performer or would like to be, it is a good idea to make your practice situation as close as possible to an actual performance. If you plan to perform standing up, then you should practice standing up. Playing the ukulele can feel a lot different when standing and if your seated position is less than perfect, your hands may be at a different angle than when sitting down.

Why Many Short Practice Sessions Are Better than a Few Long Sessions

You can learn more in a short, intense session than you can in a long, unfocused one. Your mind likes to learn things in small bits. When you're learning something new, it helps to learn in short sessions so that you can maintain a high concentration level.

Some days you will have more time to play than others. On days when time is limited, use the time to learn something new. Learn a new scale or chord, or a short, new part of a song. Then use the days when you have more time to polish the things you have learned. Repeat them until they become comfortable for you.

Eliminating Frustration

As soon as you begin to feel yourself becoming frustrated when practicing, try taking a few slow, deep breaths. This will help relieve frustration and help you to concentrate.

Usually, that feeling of frustration comes from trying to learn too much at once. You have "bitten off more than you can chew." When you feel this way, slow down a little and work on a smaller amount of material (taking a smaller bite). Practice that smaller part until you can play it easily, then take another small part and do the same thing. This will give you the sense of accomplishment that makes it fun to learn new things.

How to Tell If You're Ready to Play in a Band

If you have a wide knowledge of chords and can play in a number of positions on the fingerboard, you may be getting close to becoming a pro. If you can play lead and rhythm ukulele and do a little improvising, you're getting even closer. If you know the chords of about seven different keys and can play over a dozen songs with very few mistakes from beginning to end by memory while not losing the beat, then you may now be ready to play in a band.

How to Start a Band

There are a number of ways to find other musicians to play with. One is to ask an instructor if he/she has any students who might want to get together with you. Most instructors want to help their students find other people to play with, and they may already have some names to pass on to you. This method can help you find other ukulelists, as well as bass players, drummers, keyboard players, and singers.

Another way to find musicians to play with is to put up an ad at your local music store. Make it brief and to the point, saying what type of players you are looking for. You can place the same ad in your local newspaper or on a classified website. Many classified sections will not charge anything for this service.

How to Find and Get into an Existing Band

It's a good idea to talk to people that you know in the business and ask if they know of a band that is looking for a ukulelist. If they're not aware of any at the time, ask if they can keep you in mind and recommend you the next time they hear of an opening. You can make a personal webpage that tells about your experiences, musical preferences, and equipment. Have business cards made which include your phone number, e-mail address, and webpage address. Musicians tend to help each other, and hopefully someday you'll be in a position to return the favor.

Other ways to find bands looking for ukulelists is to, once again, look at bulletin boards in music stores and in classified ads in newspapers and online. You might also find bands that need ukulelists on the Internet.

How to Prepare for an Audition

Learning to audition well can be a huge asset to your musical career. A successful band will have several ukulelists competing for the position. Here are some tips that could make the difference between you getting the job or someone else getting it:

1. **Be well prepared.** When preparing for an audition, spend every spare minute learning the songs that you'll play at the audition. Play the songs over and over until you can play them in your sleep.

2. **Learn as much of the band's material as possible.** *Extra effort shows a good attitude and can be the reason that you are hired.* Show the band that if they were to hire you, you would be ready to start playing shows with only one or two rehearsals. In most cases, that's all there will be time for, so a successful band will need to work you in as quickly as possible.

3. **Your attitude can be as important as your playing.** The band will want to hire someone with a positive attitude, who is enthusiastic about the band and their music. When a band is looking for someone to hire, they know that they are going to be dealing with that person on a daily basis. Leave your ego at home when you are auditioning. If you are willing to relocate, be sure to tell them. This can be a major factor in the decision of whether or not to hire you.

The bottom line at an audition is that most of the time the person who gets the job is the person who wants it the most—the person with the *whatever it takes* attitude. Not all successful bands are looking for a jaded pro who has "been there, done that." A good attitude can compensate for lack of experience. Most bands are looking for members who are hungry for success. So, don't worry if you haven't played a thousand live shows or been on lots of albums. Despite your lack of experience, you could still be exactly the person they are looking for.

What You May Be Asked to Play at an Audition

At most auditions, you will be asked to play some of the band's material. You may or may not be told ahead of time which songs you will play. You may be given a few minutes with a recording of a song to see how quickly you can learn it. It's likely that you'll be asked to play some of your own material as well, so have a few things prepared that you think will fit with the style of the band. The band may very well be interested in your songwriting style as well as your playing ability and attitude.

Equipment to Bring to an Audition

Bring a spare ukulele to the audition. This way, if you should happen to break a string, everyone won't have to wait while you change it; you can just pick up your spare.

If you have a ukulele with an electronic pickup, also bring a spare instrument cable, an extension cord, and a *ground lift* (an adapter that allows you to plug a three-prong plug into a two-prong outlet). By bringing the extension cord and ground lift, you know you'll be able to plug in your amp, which is a problem you don't want to have to deal with at the start of an audition. Change your strings the day before and make sure that all of your cables work. Before your audition, make sure that all of your equipment is in good working order. This is another way to show your professionalism.

How to Be the One Everyone Wants in Their Band

1. **Show up at all rehearsals on time.** When it's time to start, have your ukulele tuned, your amp set (if you have one), and be ready to go. This shows that you are enthusiastic about playing.

2. **Learn your parts well.** Have the song arrangements memorized. Be ready to play the songs all the way through without making a lot of mistakes. Do as much preparation as possible outside of rehearsal.

3. **Have a good attitude.** Be enthusiastic about the group and about rehearsals. A positive attitude is contagious. If you're excited about playing, the other members will pick up on it and will become enthusiastic themselves.

4. **Be a team player.** Leave your ego outside the door. Keep in mind that everyone in the group is working towards a common goal. Have respect for the other members and their opinions.

5. **Help with the business of the band.** Do all you can to help promote the band, whether it's getting gigs or keeping track of the finances. Remember that being in a band is being part of a business.

6. **When you're not playing a song, don't play.** This rule applies to rehearsals, sound checks, and performances. Don't play at all between songs. Playing between songs can be distracting and annoying to other members of the group and to the audience.

7. **Never tune your ukulele out loud if you are using an amp.** Use a silent electronic tuner, one that cuts off the signal to your amp while you tune.

8. **Learn to sing.** Finding players who can sing is a big challenge for many bands. Knowing how to sing, even a little, can be the difference between you and the other person getting the job.

Your Personal Promo Pack

In order to join almost any established band, you will need to try to get an audition with that band. In order to get an audition, you may need to have your own *promo pack*. Your promo pack should contain:

- A photograph of yourself
- A recording that has two or three minutes of your best playing
- A biography that tells about your experience

Make your promo pack as professional-looking as possible by having a good photographer take your picture, and have it enlarged into an 8x10" glossy print. The recording should be one with songs that you have recorded in the studio and include parts of any songs that best demonstrate your abilities. If you can play in various styles, be sure to include them on your recording. Versatility is always a good thing.

If you haven't been in the studio, record yourself playing something at home that you can play well and shows your ability. Remember, most bands are looking for a player who can play solid rhythm ukulele as well as lead, so be sure to put something on your tape that shows you can play both. If there is a specific group for which you would like to audition, think of the kind of ukulelist that they may be looking for and make a tape especially for them.

Rehearsing and Improving the Band

Rehearsal Location

You can rehearse just about any place where you can play loudly without disturbing the neighbors. The ideal situation is one where you can leave your equipment set up and just walk in and start playing. If you can't rehearse at someone's house, look for a rehearsal facility near you. Rehearsal facilities charge by the hour, by the day, or by the month. A good way to save some money is to share the rehearsal space with another band and split the rent.

Tips for Making Rehearsals More Productive

1. **Have an agenda.** Decide on the songs to be rehearsed a few days before the rehearsal. Make sure everyone has recordings of all the relevant material.

2. **Don't be afraid to stop a song if there is a problem.** Go over the problem part a few times if necessary. Make sure everyone is clear on exactly how that part should be played.

3. **Don't beat a song into the ground by playing it over and over.** After playing a song more than a few times, it becomes easy to lose your focus. It is more productive to move on, even if you haven't perfected the song. You can come back to it a little later. This keeps rehearsals productive and also keeps the band from burning out on a particular song.

4. **Record your rehearsals.** Then listen to the recording and try to find which parts need more work. Do this as a group, if possible. This can be as productive as an actual rehearsal because the band can discuss how to fix any weak spots. It can be easier to hear the weak spots while listening to a recording than to hear them when the band is playing. It's also much easier to stop the recording than it is to stop the band in the middle of a rehearsal to make a comment.

5. **Be sure that all song intros and endings are solid.** The audience may or may not hear a mistake made during the song, but a mistake in the very beginning or at the very end of the song will be the most noticeable.

6. **Band members only at rehearsal.** The only people who should be at a rehearsal are the members of the band. Your rehearsals will be much more productive this way, because when there is even one other person in the room, the rehearsal becomes a performance. Constructive criticism between members of the band becomes more difficult because no one wants to be corrected or criticized in front of an audience.

   People outside the band will always want to watch you rehearse. Politely tell them that your band's rehearsals are *closed*. Once you have an entire show together, an open rehearsal with some invited friends can be a good opportunity to try out a live show on an audience. An open rehearsal is more of a performance than a rehearsal and should only be done when the band feels like they are ready to perform.

7. **Booking a gig is a good way to get your band members motivated.** Having a show coming up will energize the band and give everyone something to anticipate and perfect. However, be sure that the band has enough time to prepare for it.

How to Get Gigs for the Band

How Long to Rehearse Before You Play Your First Gig

Before you play your first gig, you should have rehearsed the songs until you are just starting to get bored playing them. If you know a song that well, then you know it well enough to play it live. The band will probably be somewhat nervous during its first performance. The more automatic the songs are, the fewer chances there are of making mistakes due to nerves.

Getting Ready for the Gig

The more prepared you are for a show, the more fun you'll have. You will be able to focus on enjoying yourself as well as focusing on what you are playing. You will always play your best when you don't have to think about what you're playing.

The Band's Promo Pack

In order for your band to get gigs you will need to have a *promo pack* for the band. This is different from your own personal promo pack that we discussed on page 107. Your band's promo pack should include the following:

1. **A recording of the band.** If your band has a CD or an MP3 recording on a disc drive, include one in your promo pack. If it doesn't, record three of your best songs and include the recording in your promo pack. Club owners won't want to spend a lot of time listening to your demo, so three songs will be plenty.

2. **A photo of the band.** You can either get creative here or have a simple photo of the band. If you choose to get creative, be sure that the photo reflects the style of music that you play.

3. **A brief history of the band, including:**
   A. A description of the style of music that the band plays.
   B. The names of the band members and what instruments they play.
   C. A list of songs the band plays.
   D. A list of places the band has played before.
   E. Anything interesting about the band.

4. **Any newspaper article, review, or press about the band.** Good press or reviews about the band are a great addition to your promo pack. Photocopy any articles or photographs, and include the name and date of the newspaper or magazine in which they appeared.

5. **The name and number of the businessperson for the band.** For example, "For booking and information, contact John Smith at (555) 555-5555." *Be sure that this number is given in several places in the promo pack*, especially on the recording package and on the photo. In case parts of the kit get separated, people will still be able to contact you. You will need to have an answering machine for your contact number so that the person who may want to book your band can leave a message. Remember that your promo pack reflects your band and its professionalism.

How to Use a Promo Pack

Give copies of your *promo pack* to the managers of clubs or other places where your band could play. It's also a good idea to give copies to *booking agents*, because a good booking agent will be able to find you more gigs than you would be able to find on your own. The booking agent will charge a fee for each gig that he/she books. This may be a flat fee or a percentage of what the band is paid. You should also give copies of your promo pack to magazines and newspapers; they may want to do a review or a story on your band.

The Gig

How to Get Ready Backstage

Here's a routine that will help you warm up and get in the right frame of mind to perform. Start with stretching until you feel limber. Then start warming up on your ukulele. Play chords, licks, and scales, starting slowly and gradually speeding up until your hands feel loose and ready to go. Don't go overboard, though. You could fatigue your hands before the show, which defeats the purpose of warming up. You may be nervous before a performance. Deep breathing and stretching exercises can be helpful for overcoming pre-performance jitters.

Words to Keep in Mind to Help Give Your Best Performance

Instead of thinking, "let me *impress* the audience," think, "let me *entertain* the audience." Your main job when you're performing live is to have fun and to entertain the audience. If you are having fun and are playing like there's no place you would rather be than on stage, your audience will pick up on that attitude and enjoy watching you play.

What to Do if You Make a Mistake

There are two kinds of mistakes: arrangement mistakes and playing mistakes. An arrangement mistake is when a player forgets how the song is supposed to be played and, for example, plays the wrong section of the song at the wrong time. Arrangement mistakes are usually more noticeable and are a sign that the song still needs some work. If you know your songs well, you shouldn't be making these kinds of errors.

A playing mistake is when a player plays the wrong note or chord. These mistakes are a basic part of life—even the best players make them from time to time—and are usually easy to cover up. However, if you are making more than one playing mistake every few songs, you may want to practice your parts on your own, just to refresh them in your mind.

If you make a mistake when you're performing, just relax and jump back into the song. Try not to make a face or do anything that would let the audience know that you made a mistake. Chances are, unless the mistake is really obvious, no one will even notice. Don't dwell on it, just continue on with the song as if it never happened. Thinking about a mistake after you make it will only distract you and cause you to make even more mistakes.

How to Make Your Mistakes Less Noticeable

It's normal to make mistakes, but one thing you can do to make your mistakes less obvious is to play right through them. The way to practice this is to pretend you are performing. Play the song from start to finish and play right through any mistakes you might make. When you are playing by yourself, you may be tempted to stop when you make a mistake. Try to resist this temptation. The golden rule of performing is this: *No matter what happens, don't stop during the song.* When you are practicing a song from start to finish, follow this rule just as you would during a performance.

Practice Playing the Songs Without Looking

The less you look at your ukulele, the more eye contact you can have with the audience. Playing the songs without looking shows that you have confidence in what you are doing. However, there are certain times when you should look at your ukulele. For example, when you are shifting from one part of the fingerboard to another, it is better to watch where you are going than to make the jump without looking, which could cause you to land on the wrong fret. After you practice without looking for a while, you'll start to get a feel for where the notes are on the fingerboard.

The information in this section, which started on page 102, is from *The Pro Guitarist's Handbook* (#19426), which contains many more great tips on being a professional musician and is available at your local music dealer, online retailer, and alfred.com.

Notes

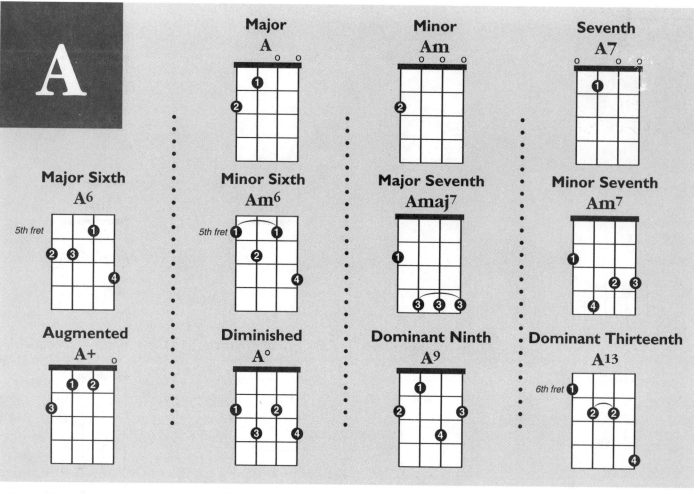

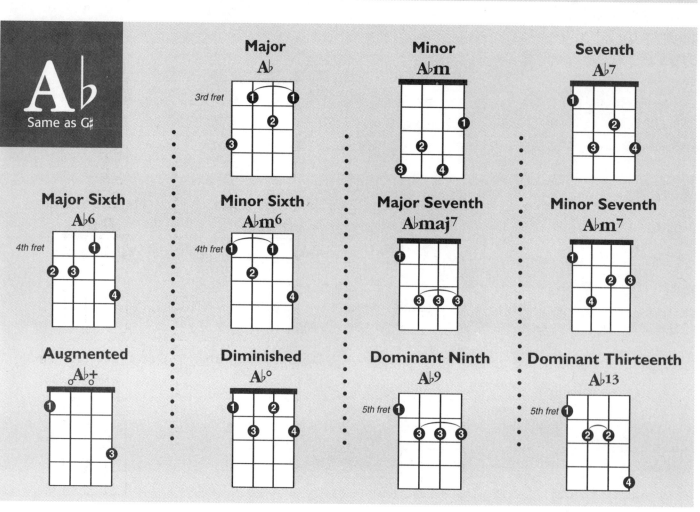

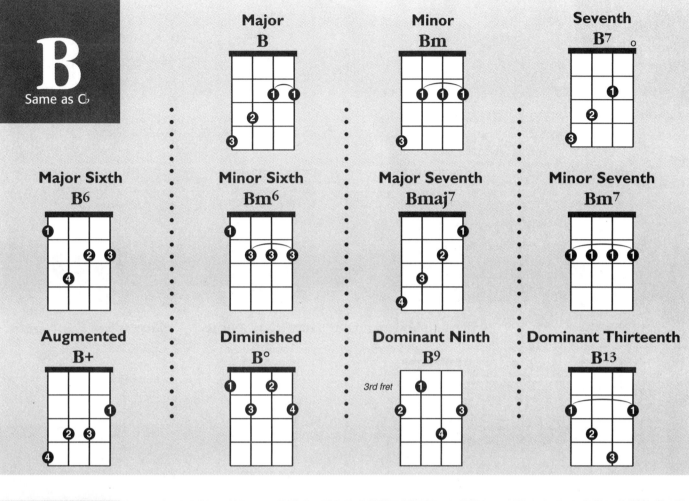

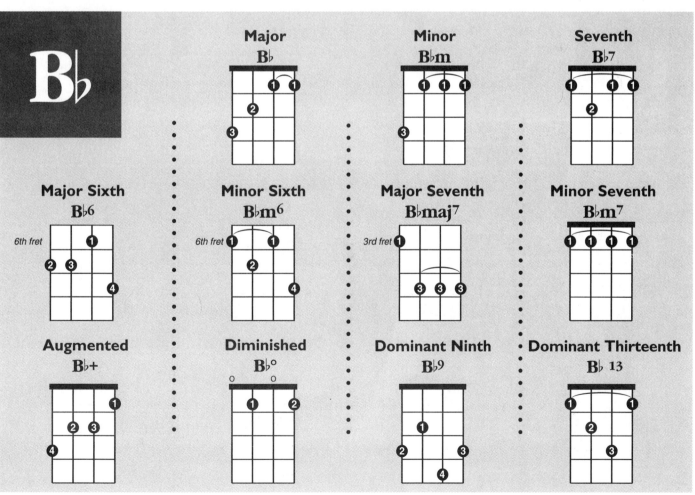

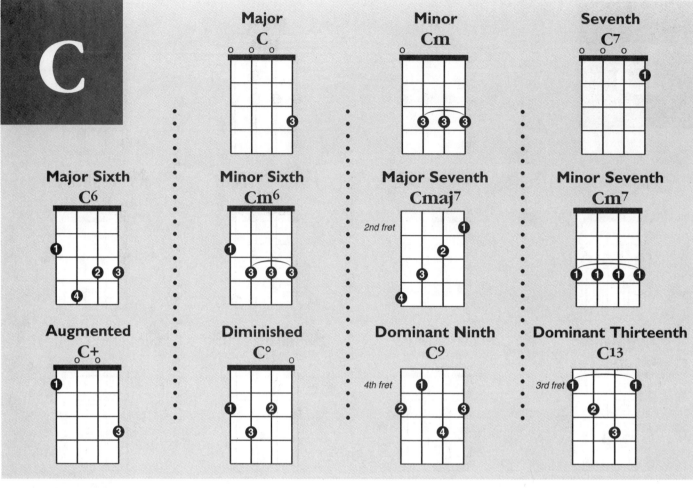

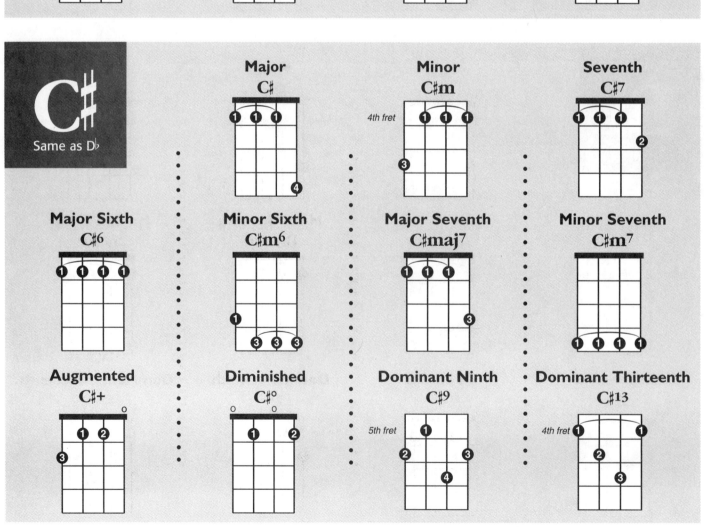

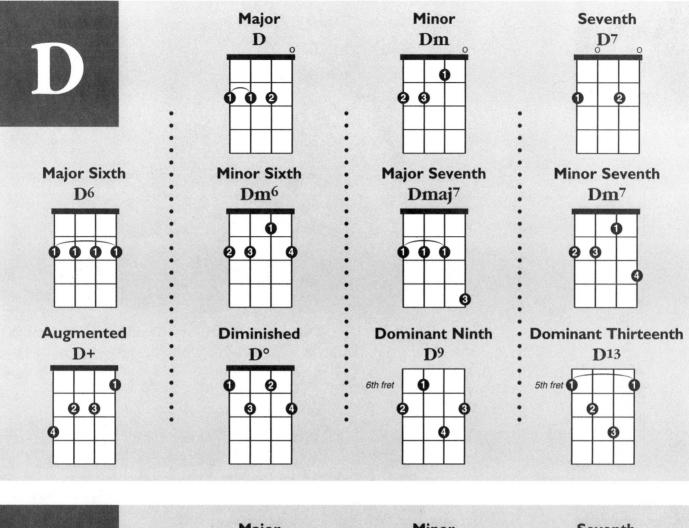

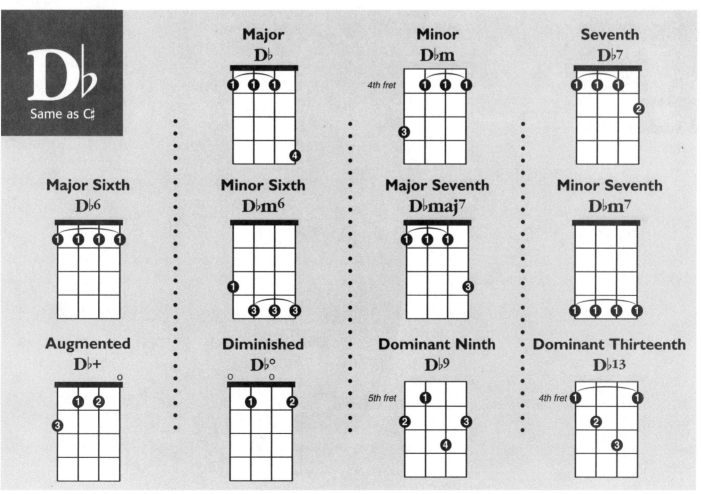

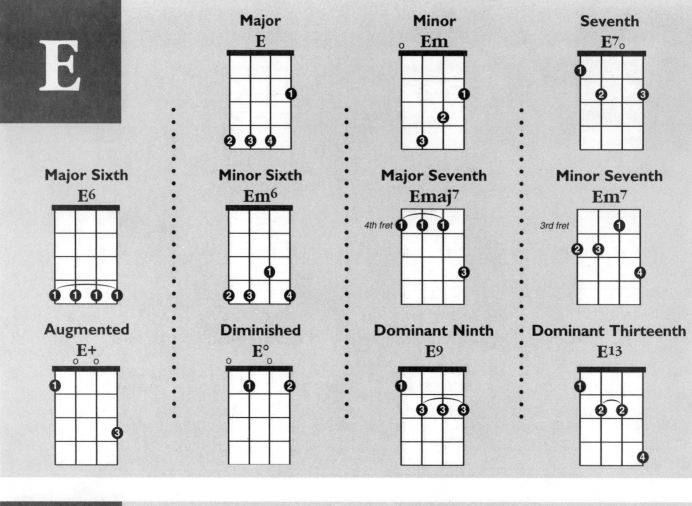

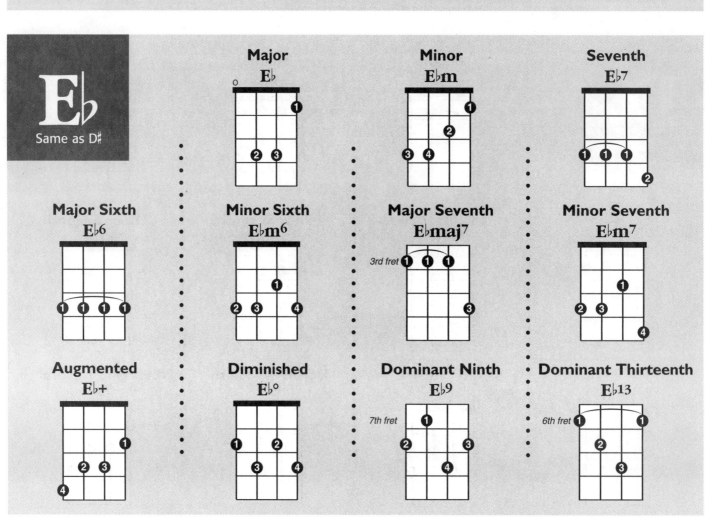

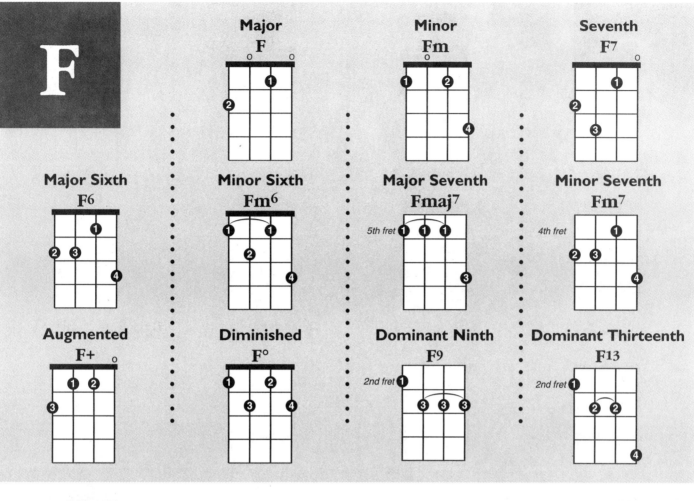

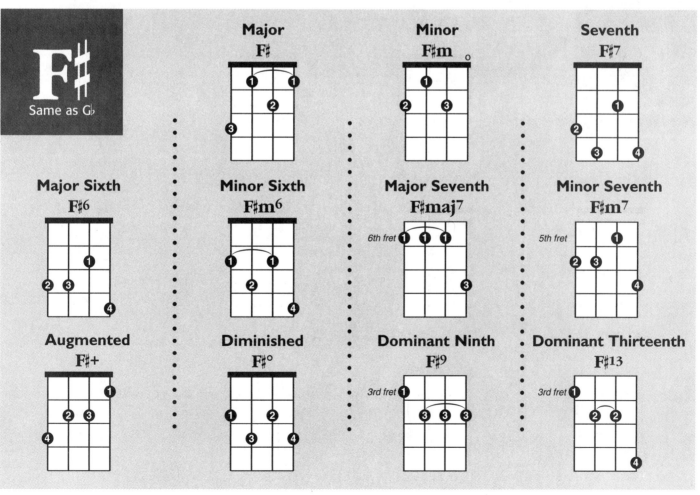

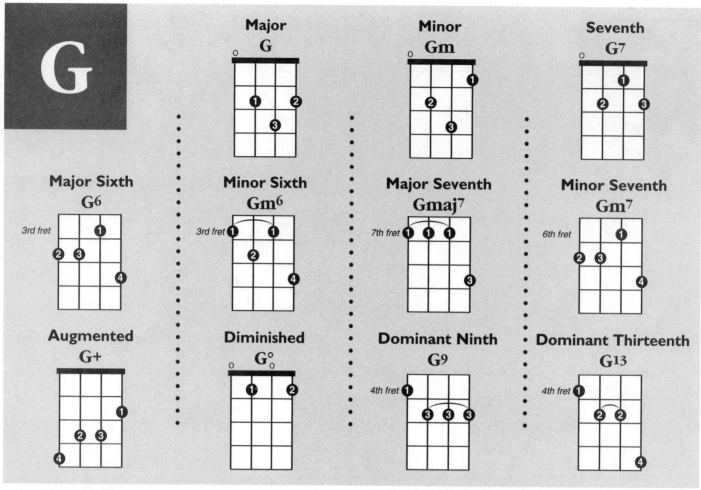

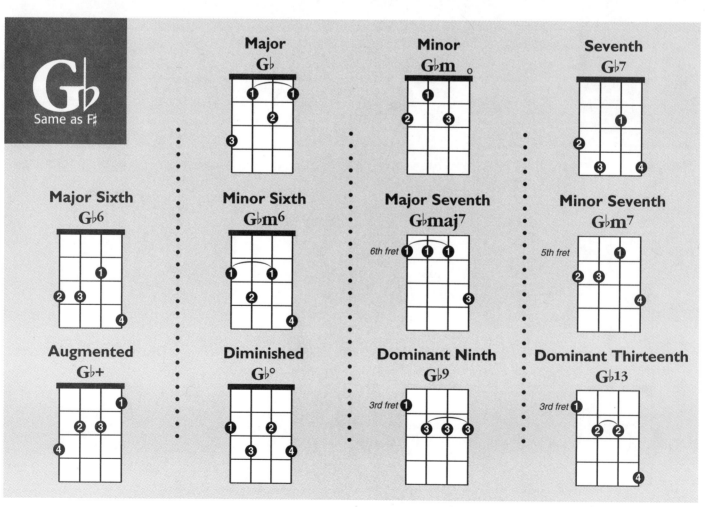

Notes

Ukulele Fingerboard Chart
Frets 1–12

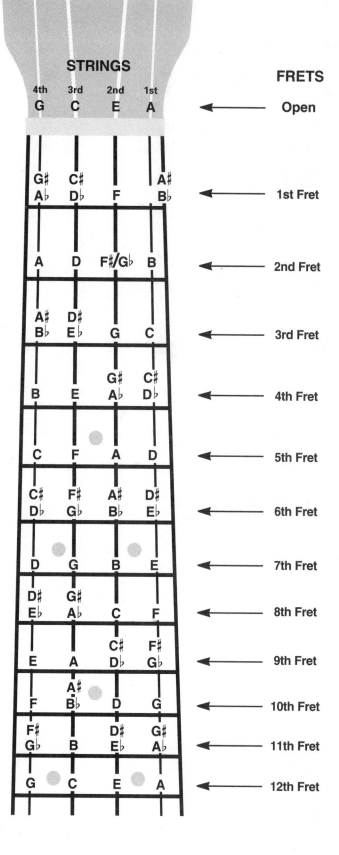

STRINGS

4th	3rd	2nd	1st
G	C	E	A

FRETS

	Fret
←	Open
←	1st Fret
←	2nd Fret
←	3rd Fret
←	4th Fret
←	5th Fret
←	6th Fret
←	7th Fret
←	8th Fret
←	9th Fret
←	10th Fret
←	11th Fret
←	12th Fret

4th (G)	3rd (C)	2nd (E)	1st (A)	
G	C	E	A	Open
G#/Ab	C#/Db	F	A#/Bb	1st Fret
A	D	F#/Gb	B	2nd Fret
A#/Bb	D#/Eb	G	C	3rd Fret
B	E	G#/Ab	C#/Db	4th Fret
C	F	A	D	5th Fret
C#/Db	F#/Gb	A#/Bb	D#/Eb	6th Fret
D	G	B	E	7th Fret
D#/Eb	G#/Ab	C	F	8th Fret
E	A	C#/Db	F#/Gb	9th Fret
F	A#/Bb	D	G	10th Fret
F#/Gb	B	D#/Eb	G#/Ab	11th Fret
G	C	E	A	12th Fret